W9-DGH-946

Conflicting Images of Man

Conflicting Images of Man

Edited by
WILLIAM NICHOLLS

Library
Southwestern State College
Weatherford

The Seabury Press
NEW YORK

ACKNOWLEDGMENTS

Grateful acknowledgment is ▓▓▓ to the following publishers for permission to use copyrighted m▓▓▓ ▓▓▓ the titles listed:

Columbia University Press—Ja▓▓▓ B. Conant, *M▓▓▓* ▓▓▓ *and Modern Man*.

Harcourt, Brace & World, Inc.—T. S. Eliot, "Ash Wednesday" and "East Coker" in *The Complete Poems and Plays, 1909–1962*.

Harper & Row—Pierre Teilhard de Chardin, *The Divine Milieu, Letters from a Traveller,* and *The Phenomenon of Man*.

Copyright © 1966 by The Seabury Press, Incorporated
Library of Congress Catalog Card Number: 64-19627
DESIGN BY CAROL BASEN BAILYN
517-1165-C
Printed in the United States of America

Preface

233
N51c

The contributors to this volume are at one in supposing that the Christian theological tradition has still a contribution to offer to the discussion of what it means to be a human being in our time. There is no need to regard them as constituting a close unity in other respects. We do not aspire to be a new theological school of thought, and most of us would believe that this is not an appropriate time for the formation of such schools and lobbies. Several of the contributors, so far as I am aware, have never met each other, and the responsibility for their appearance between the same covers must be assigned to the Editor, who is in general the link between them. Of the theologians among us, it may be said that we all believe that any reformulation of the doctrine of man in our own time must, as in the past, be carried on in dialogue with the thought of the secular world. Although we may differ in the extent to which we believe reconstruction is in fact called for, and in evaluating the current condition of man, we agree on what has been termed the relevance of the secular. It is in part for such reasons that I have solicited a contribution from Professor D. G. Brown, of the Philosophy Department of my own University, who views the activities of Christians,

97809 v

whether theologians or not, from the standpoint of a not un-
sympathetic but certainly an external observer. Although our
essays appear under the imprint of an Anglican publishing
house, and the Editor himself happens to be an Anglican,
most of the contributors are not.

It remains to thank the Editor of The Seabury Press,
Arthur R. Buckley, for suggesting the theme of the book, for
valuable criticism along the way, and for patient endurance
of the unforeseen delays that not seldom beset a cooperative
enterprise of this type, and which we have not failed to encounter. For the remaining deficiencies of the book, its
Editor is primarily responsible.

William Nicholls

UNIVERSITY OF BRITISH COLUMBIA
May, 1965

Contents

Editor's Introduction

We live in a time of ferment over Christian doctrine more intense, perhaps, than any since that which accompanied the emergence of the Church from Judaism. In such a ferment all Christian doctrines find themselves under criticism, from the doctrine of God to ethics. Perhaps the doctrine of God is the one which has undergone the most radical reformulation at the hands of some of our contemporaries,* but in the sphere of ethics a striking reassessment of Christian practice is taking place. The *Honest to God* debate has shown that in the English-speaking world a large public continues to be interested in the discussion of theological issues, provided that the issues are felt to touch upon people's real problems. That debate† has largely dealt with the doctrines just referred to, those of the nature of God and the character and content of Christian ethics. It is the conviction of the contributors to the present volume that the doctrine of man is equally worthy of attention from a public, whether theological or lay, that is

* See, e.g., Paul Van Buren, *The Secular Meaning of the Gospel* (New York: The Macmillan Co., 1963).

† See J. A. T. Robinson, *Honest to God* (London: S.C.M. Press, 1963); J. A. T. Robinson and David L. Edwards (eds.), *The Honest to God Debate* (London: S.C.M. Press, 1963); and Alasdair MacIntyre, "God and the Theologians," *Encounter* (Sept., 1963), also reprinted, in shorter form, in *The Honest to God Debate*.

concerned to discover the form of Christian faith in the second half of the twentieth century.

If the doctrine of man is not at the center of Christian theology, it will readily be agreed that it lies within its central region. Perhaps none of the contributors to this volume would commit himself to the famous dictum "theology is anthropology," * and several would presumably prefer to join those who see Christology as the foundation of other Christian doctrines. But if that is how things are, as I have endeavored to point out in my own concluding essay, anthropology does not simply depend upon Christology, but reciprocally influences it through the presuppositions about man that are brought to the construction of a Christology, and thus in turn influences all other doctrines. More broadly, of course, no apology need be made for continuing the inquiry into what it means to be a human being in our time.

What remains to be said about man, from a Christian point of view, after the systematic theologians of the past and present have done their work? Clearly, in our view, something, or no justification could be offered for what we have done. Systematic theology, the intellectual formulation of the faith of Christians, needs to be done again in every age, and the more frequently as the pace of change accelerates. Already we are finding that the great men whose seminal thinking was done in the thirties, and who have now retired, or are on the point of retirement from active theological work, no longer fully satisfy us with their formulations. What will satisfy us is not yet clear, at least to us. We are not ourselves ready, perhaps never will be ready, to create massive systems of theology in the manner of a Barth, a Tillich, or a Brunner.

* Professor Brown, writing as one who is not a Christian, is inclined to allot to anthropology those theological doctrines that he does not find vacuous.

But we think we have something to say which may contribute toward the eventual emergence of more confident Christian utterance.

The plan of the present book reflects these concerns and attitudes. The first essay, by Professor Nathan A. Scott, Jr., sketches once more the traditional Christian understanding of man against the background of the intuitions of modern man about himself as reflected in literature and the plastic arts. Scott's essay was written first, and shown to the other contributors before their own essays were written. It thus provides a point of reference for the remaining essays, which in one way or another assume the fact, if not the necessity, of reformulation.

The second essay, by Professor Ronald Gregor Smith, deals with post-Renaissance man, that is, with the man of today, whose historical origins lie, in the view of the author, above all in the assertion of human autonomy and potential secularity at the time of the Renaissance. Yet, as Gregor Smith shows, man today is not rightly understood simply as the inheritor of a confident or even brash claim of unlimited human possibilities. He is also the one who knows that he stands on the brink of destruction, a possibility arising out of the exercise of this very autonomy. In consequence he experiences, in a phrase that we have adapted as our general title, a conflict of images of himself.

One of the ways of thought about man most characteristic of our time is that which approaches him from the outside, as an object of research. The next contributor, Professor James M. Gustafson, accordingly offers a study of man in the light of social science and of Christian faith. He discusses three assumptions of social science, that behavior is determined, that man is the creature of needs and desires, and that behavior is researchable. In the light of Christian faith these are novel, and perhaps in the last resort inadequate, assumptions, but Gustafson recognizes the extent to which evidence affords them empirical justification.

In the next essay, Professor K. R. Bridston examines a number of secular views of man in the light of faith in Christ. He does not believe that the theologian ought to adopt a defensive posture in the face of great secular thinkers like Darwin, Marx, and Freud. A Christian critique of such writers must instead, he thinks, be based on an attitude of repentance and humility, and therefore of willingness to learn what they can teach. Nor does the Christian, in Bridston's view, have the task of offering alternative views of man to supplant the secular views. What he must offer is Jesus Christ, the "proper man," in the confidence that all that is true in the secular anthropologies will be taken up and integrated in Christ.

Professor D. G. Brown, in what is in certain respects a companion piece, offers a secular challenge to Christian views of man. This challenge is nonetheless radical for being couched in urbane terms, for it amounts to this, that Christians have failed to make out a view of man: Whatever in Christian anthropology does not turn out in the light of analysis to be vacuous can be taken over for its own by secular anthropology. There remains nothing distinctive for secular man to come to terms with. So far as these contentions are based on an analysis of religious language, they come under discussion in my own concluding essay.

The next two essays are also in a sense companion pieces. They treat descriptively two possible Christian solutions to the problem of understanding man today. Professor Pieter de Jong deals with the thought of the Jesuit paleontologist Teilhard de Chardin, whose ideas, since their publication, have interested very diverse people. De Jong gives us an ac-

count of Teilhard's view of man as the spearhead of the evolutionary process, whose end is in God. Professor R. H.
Fuller, the original translator of Bonhoeffer's *Letters and
Papers from Prison,* takes a second look at one of the most
important and frequently misunderstood of Bonhoeffer's
ideas, that of the maturity of the world, or the coming of
age of man. He shows that even in its fragmentary expression, Bonhoeffer's thought on this theme is not open to some
of the objections that are commonly leveled against it, and
that it does not lack subtlety and discretion.

In a final essay, the Editor endeavors to sum up the themes
of the book in a critical look at an idea which has so far
seemed to him well founded, the dependence of a doctrine
of man upon a doctrine of Christ. He endeavors to show that
Christology must be more concerned with the historical question of what Jesus was actually like than many influential
contemporary theologians have been willing to allow, and
that this concern is relevant to Christian anthropology as well
as to Christology. He then turns, through an analysis of
theological language, to the question, first raised by Bonhoeffer, and lately put in striking form by Paul Van Buren,
of how God and Christ may be understood in a secular (or
"religionless") way. He concludes that only by solving these
questions will it be possible to speak of God at all in the
world that is now coming into being, but that an examination
of the relationship between theological language and Christology shows that something meaningful is being asserted
when Christians speak of God, and that they have, therefore,
something distinctive to say about man. In a final section, he
makes use of ideas drawn in part from Bonhoeffer and Tillich
to speak of the relationship of a believing secular man to God.

1

The Christian Understanding of Man

by Nathan A. Scott, Jr.

To attempt at the present time, however unsystematically, to reflect on what theologians call "the Christian doctrine of man" is for one immediately to be put in mind of the sharp difference between the traditional Christian perspective and that vision of things which we recognize as characteristically modern. If our art and literature and philosophy are consulted for clues as to the basic stress of the age, it would seem that, nearly half a millennium after Copernicus, man is again suffering such a sense of diminution as was first spoken of as "Copernican." For in such representative expressions of our period-style as Kafka's *Der Prozess*, Heidegger's *Sein und Zeit*, Picasso's *Guernica*, Brecht's *Mutter Courage und Ihre Kinder*, Sartre's *L'Être et le Néant*, Camus' *L'Étranger*, and Beckett's *En attendant Godot*, the human image that is projected is something like those doomed ghosts, in the pictures of the contemporary English painter Francis Bacon, who look out at the world heart-stricken and aghast. Or it is like a face described by the English writer Alex Comfort. In his novel *On This Side Nothing* is a sentence which says: "I saw the same fear in her face that I should have felt if a stranger called at night, the world-wide twentieth-century

7

fear which one sees wherever one knocks unexpectedly at any door."

Indeed, all those artists and poets and philosophers who are recording today in a distinctively contemporary idiom man's traumatic encounter with himself are forging an image of the human creature as one ousted from the precincts of stability and grace and order and security, as one who has no place of safety and whose being is therefore "porous . . . like those cryptic human figures in modern sculpture that are full of holes or gaps." [1] The German philosopher Helmut Kuhn entitled his study of existentialism *Encounter with Nothingness,* and it would be difficult to come by any other phrase that so concisely renders the spiritual drama that is consistently enacted in the most representative philosophy and literature and visual art of our time. The protagonists in these records of modern sensibility are creatures "full of holes and gaps, faceless, riddled with doubts and negations, starkly finite" [2]—and, in their porousness, they are at the point of being invaded by the surrounding Nothingness. Perhaps the ideogram that most perfectly depicts the changed presence of man is the cipher.

This sense of man's impoverishment and utter indigence that today so deeply informs a widely prevalent mood does not, of course, spring from any merely willful inclination toward Manichaean styles of imagination. It is rather, in part, a consequence of our feeling overwhelmed by the ambiguous results of our own creativity. By virtue of the political and scientific instrumentalities that have been fashioned by what Paul Tillich calls "technical reason," [3] we find ourselves living in a world whose potential explosiveness infinitely surpasses any of the dangers that in one period or another have figured in man's recorded past. And, in this perilous time, there has arisen a crisis of confidence in our ability successfully to manage the arena of history. In the presence of a scientific establishment that has ushered in the nuclear age and in the presence of a political establishment that generates so much frightening tension in the world community, we feel that, like Mary Shelley's Frankenstein, we may have created a "second nature"[4] which is beyond our capacity to control. And, far more profoundly even, the sense of human life as totally contingent and as therefore exposed to the invading pressures of Nothingness is today a result of that general collapse of confidence in the authenticity of traditional religious faith which undoubtedly constitutes the basic loss underlying all the other losses felt by the men and women of our age.

But, however one accounts for what is presently negative in the human image that drifts throughout our literature and art and philosophy, its nihilistic bleakness is not to be gainsaid and does in fact invite the Christian community—in whose remembrance of Jesus Christ there is enshrined quite a different vision of the human prospect—to plot the possibility of heightening and deepening man's estimate of himself in this late stage of modern experience. Which is of course to say that in the field of what is called "anthropology," Christian thought has today a very distinct mission, even— let us say it—an evangelical mission. This must not be forgotten during the present period of theological realignment, when we are by way of discovering "the secular meaning of the Gospel"[5] and our vocation to a "religionless Christianity." The late Dietrich Bonhoeffer has, to be sure, taught us to understand that the world has "come of age"—and so it has, in the sense of having discarded "the religious premise," the old supranaturalist notion, that is, of God as *deus ex machina,* as *a* Being "above" or "beyond" the world, whose "existence" is a matter of theoretical knowledge. But never for a moment did Bonhoeffer suppose that the mutation in modern intellectual history betokened by the decline of "the religious premise" was a development entailing some great new advance in moral and spiritual maturity. And this his more ardent disciples occasionally appear not to be remembering when they permit their eagerness for "dialogue" with "modern man" to mislead them into performing so drastic a surgery on the Christian message as to rob it of the possibility of bringing a prophetic and renewing evangel into our broken and unhappy world.

Indeed, it is just at the point where we begin to contemplate the status, the basic predicament, and the ultimate vocation of man that the Christian gospel, if deeply listened to, may lead the modern imagination toward a genuine catharsis. For, far from being any kind of faceless cipher, man is disclosed in the Christian story about reality to be a creature "trailing clouds of glory." The *doxa* or "glory" of God is, in the perspectives of biblical thought, that *dynamis,* that power, that creative energy, by which whatever exists is called into existence: and man is declared to be made in the image of this "glory." This is to say that he is a radically theological being: he is "open" to the ineffable mystery of the Ground of being: the light of his being is (as it is so beautifully said by Hans Urs von Balthasar[6]) "a dialogical light," for in the basic constitution of his nature he is turned toward God, and in Christian experience the God whom he meets is turned toward him. In other words, in the Christian understanding of man, the *humanum,* the specifically human thing in us, requires definition in terms of what Schleiermacher called the "absolute dependence" in which man lives with respect to God: he is made "in the image of God" (Gen. 1:26): we do indeed "reflect as in a mirror the splendour of the Lord; [and] thus we are trans-

figured into his likeness, from splendour to splendour" (II
Cor. 3:18, NEB)—"from glory to glory." To be human is, in
short, to be stamped by and to bear the imprint in oneself
of the glory of God.

Although "trailing clouds of glory," man does not, however, in the Christian sense of things, enjoy any self-sufficiency. For he is of the earth, earthy; and his flesh, like all
flesh, says the Bible, is grass—which, with the passage of time,
fades and withers away. He is, in short, a creature; and his
finitude is ineluctable. He must have air to breathe; he needs
space in which to abide; if he cannot find warmth and nourishment, he will perish; yet, even with plentifulness of what
are called "creature comforts," his life is but of short duration, for it is bracketed within the consecutive flow of tem-
porality and is indeed a kind of running-toward-death. *Le
temps humain* comes to us, in other words, as passing and
perishing—and although we sing in our chains like the sea,
said Dylan Thomas, Time holds us green and dying.* We
are but the merest reeds in nature, and nothing stays for us:
there is no escaping what Camus called "the cruel mathematics that command our condition." And "which of you
by taking thought can add one cubit to his stature?" (Matt.
6:27) Even after taking thought, even in the highest reaches
of the mind's transcendence of itself and of its world, man
remains a being (in Unamuno's phrase) "of flesh and bone"
whose life is imbedded in the contingencies of nature and
the relativities of history: his perspectives, in other words,
are always partial and limited and conditioned by the particular time and place that he happens to occupy. And thus
Augustine was led to declare that "all who maintain that

* I have paraphrased the last two lines of Thomas's "Fern Hill."
See Dylan Thomas, *The Collected Poems* (New York: New Directions,
1953), p. 180.

our progress is to be so complete that we shall be changed
into the substance of God, and that we shall thus become
what He is should look well to it how they build up their
opinion; upon myself I must confess that it produces no
conviction." [7]

Yet, though the reality of man in the ontological order is
ineradicably creatural, "the fact that, through reason and
memory and imagination, he can surmount himself and his
world indeterminately means that his life cannot find its
true ground in any of the proximate norms that emerge out
of historical experience, and that he is therefore driven by
the inner dynamism of his nature toward a transcendent
norm." [8] He is, in short, "open" to God: wrought into the
essential fiber of his nature is the very "image" of God, and
his status under God is that of "sonship."

The sonship that man bears with respect to God is, however, in the Christian estimate of his conditions, something
that is known to have been trespassed against and broken.
"The way of man is not in himself" (Jer. 10:23), and our
hearts are restless till they find their rest in God: as it was
put by Dante, in one of the great sentences of Western poetry,
E'n la sua voluntate è nostra pace ("In His will is our peace").
But the actuality of human life discloses man's existential
condition to be one of estrangement and alienation from the
true ground of his being.

No Christian thinker of the modern period, and perhaps
in the entire theological tradition, has argued the contention
so powerfully as the distinguished theologian of Basel, Karl
Barth, that in the perspective of the Christian faith the most
decisive manifestation of the "real" man is to be encountered
in Jesus Christ. Here it is, as Barth has told us in one after
another of his massive treatises, here it is, in the man of
Galilee, that Christianity meets what is for it the definitive

disclosure both of man's essential nature and of how all men would live were they to give full expression to that nature. And what Jesus of Nazareth most unmistakably reveals is that it is man's vocation to live "with God as His covenant-partner." [9] Indeed, says Barth, "the divinity of the man Jesus is to be described comprehensively in the statement that He is man for God." [10] But, since man belongs to the creatural order, for him to be *for* God is for him to be for the *things* of God, for God's *creatures:* his commitment is to the life of encounter, and the line that is taken in Barth's *Church Dogmatics* is the line that Gabriel Marcel is taking in his Gifford Lectures, when he says: ". . . the more my existence takes on the character of including others, the narrower becomes the gap which separates it from *being;* the more, in other words, I am." [11] Thus for Christian anthropology, the "real" man is, as Barth puts it, "the man for other men."

The kind of norm that is embodied in the New Testament picture of Jesus as the Christ is, however, consistently contradicted in human life. And what seems everywhere and always to have been *actually* normative among men is a deeply ingrained self-centeredness, generating exploitativeness and envy and mistrust toward the neighbor. Man is created in the image of God, made for covenant-partnership with God and for fellowship with his human neighbors; but he is a good thing spoiled, a creature radically evil, who changes "the glory of the incorruptible God into an image made like unto corruptible man" (Rom. 1:23). With his characteristic conciseness Pascal defines the matter in this way: "This I is hateful. . . . In one word it has two qualities: It is essentially unjust in that it makes self the centre of everything and it is troublesome to others in that it seeks to make them subservient; for each I is the enemy and would be the tyrant of all others." [12]

This congenital crookedness and illiberality of the human heart has never been extenuated in the classical traditions of Christian theology. Indeed, it is just this dimension of things which makes for a second major principle of Christian anthropology; for it is held not only that man is created in the image of God, for covenant-partnership with him in the continuous work of creation, but also that, through his pride and unfaith, man has become alienated from God and thus lives in bondage to sin. Biblically, the classic statement of this taint of human nature is the myth of the Fall in the Book of Genesis; and, in theological tradition, the classic formulation is expressed in the dogma of Original Sin. But, of course, in neither case are we being offered a *chronological* description of how it has come to be that human life is stained by the improbities and corruptions of sin. In the case of the Genesis story of the Garden of Eden, we are not dealing with a place to be spotted on a map of the Middle East or with an occurrence that is datable on any historical calendar; nor is it proper so to historicize the dogma of Original Sin as to convert it into a formula of the natural history of sin and of the biological inheritance of an original corruption. No: on the contrary, Christian thought has long since come to understand that both formulations are mythical statements of the profound contradiction in which human life is caught. For, though he is so created that "the law of his nature is love, a harmonious relation of life to life in obedience to the divine centre and source of his life," man does persist in refusing "to acknowledge himself as merely a member of a total unity of life," and thus, in Reinhold Niebuhr's words, "he is betrayed by his very ability to survey the whole to imagine himself the whole." [13] He is a *fallen* creature, in other words, because, although (as P. T. Forsyth said [14]) he inherits greatness and inhabits promise, he lives in a state of disharmony with what is the essential law of his nature; and to speak of the *originality* of his sin is to speak of its tragically disruptive presence in every moment of experience, of the fact that human existence is consistently and pervasively characterized by man's alienation from God and by the tensions that are introduced into the human community by man's habitual egocentricity.

Christianity has, then, a quite special definition of what the popular existentialism of our day, with a thrilling shiver of nervousness, likes to call "the human predicament." For, in its purview, the things of human life, contrary to the assumption of both Rousseau and Marx, are not thrown into disarray by the inertia of social and political institutions and the "cultural lag"; nor does Christian anthropology follow that tradition of thought (anciently expressed in Socratic humanism) which has perennially located the seat of the human problem in man's ignorance; and it is quite impossible to accommodate with genuinely Christian perspectives the various modern theories which tell us in effect that man's basic difficulty stems from vestigial remnants of animal impulse and from the "evolutionary lag." Christianity, instead, insists that the real source of man's most serious troubles is to be found not outside himself nor in some special aspect of human selfhood but, rather, at the very center of human personality. Man's profoundest unhappiness and dispeace are caused, in the analysis of Christian theology, because he *will not* live in obedience to the divinely ordained law of his being—which is the law of love. In other words, the heart of our trouble, in the Christian estimate, lies (as it is put in the classic language of Martin Luther) in the "bondage of the will." Perhaps this is to say, as Kierkegaard suggests,[15] that sin posits or presupposes itself. It is not, as some theologians have suggested, that the human condition is one of Total Corruption, in the sense of conforming to Thomas Hobbes's description of it as "poor, nasty, [and] brutish." But what is true of man's situation is that the disorders which his pride and self-centeredness have introduced into life so permeate the whole range of his experience that he cannot, merely by an act of will, liberate himself from self-regarding styles of thought and imagination; indeed, we are joined and ingrafted into one another in our sin. As John Seldon Whale says, "Your failure matches mine and our lives interlock to form an organic system of evil."[16] And from this captivity we do not effect our own release.

In exploring the question as to how sin is ultimately to be accounted for, Whale has also remarked how easily the alleged explanations of the fact that all men sin do themselves tend to become a kind of determinism which treats sin not as a moral fact but as a natural fact. "Determine the causes of a universal moral fact," he says, "and it ceases to be moral," [17] for, inevitably, as it becomes one integer in a complex chain of causation, the element of personal responsibility and freedom is removed; and, of course, apart from freedom and responsibility the very idea of sin is inconceivable. Then, with a brilliant pungency Whale reminds us:

The attempt to trace sin back to an empirical fact which causes it, invalidates man's God-given sense that he is a will and a person. The will is *ex hypothesi* that which is non-derivable. Man's sinful will cannot be explained: it must remain as the one completely irrational fact in a world which God created, and saw to be "very good." [18]

But, despite Christianity's acute sense of man as a creature flawed by his own perversity and incapable of delivering himself from his deepest woe, it is surely a mistake to suppose (as a certain kind of theological radicalism of the present time often seems to) that Christianity is equivalent to "the tragic sense of life." It is undoubtedly true, of course, that a thinker like Karl Jaspers is quite wrong in contending that the relation between the tragic principle and the Christian faith is flatly antithetical.[19] For the whole point and meaning of Calvary is that, when a True Man entered our midst, his goodness, his sinlessness, had so rankling an effect on such men as ourselves that he was finally nailed to a cross. Here it is that the distempers which break our peace and sanity and which frustrate even God's purposes—here it is that they are most fully revealed. To quote H. R. MacKintosh: "What sin really is—its rebellion, malignancy, and horror— could never be completely detected or revealed while it was being committed against those who themselves shared the imperfection of the sinner." [20] But the cross of Christ brings it all home to us, for we can see ourselves in the *personae* of the drama that was enacted at the Place of a Skull; and it is a tragic drama because it discloses that, by reason of the callousness and complacency and self-deceptiveness and treachery of men very much like ourselves, a completely divine life was made to taste the gall of slander and persecution, of rejection and sympathy withdrawn, and was finally blasted into death and silence.

Yet, though "the tragic sense of life" is absorbed into the Christian vision, Christianity does finally stand "beyond tragedy." For the tragic *mystique* sees reality as riven and at cross-purposes with itself, as direly strained by antinomies both ontological and moral that are unconciliable: the Italian novelist Ignazio Silone says that "in the sacred history of man on earth, it is still, alas, Good Friday," [21] and this is indeed the judgment to which we must be brought by a consistently tragic outlook on the human prospect. But things are at last seen quite differently from the perspective of the Christian faith. And thus we are brought to a third major principle of Christian anthropology, which not only asserts that man is created in the image of God and that he has "fallen" into alienation from God, but which also asserts that God has resources surpassing ours: for allaying man's woe, for reconstituting what is broken in our humanity, and (as it is put in the *Agnus Dei* of the Mass) for taking away the sin of the world.

Ecce agnus dei, ecce qui tollit peccata mundi: here is indeed the central message of the New Testament, that he in whom there was no sin was "made sin" for us and that the agony of Jesus on the Tree—"Christ crucified"—is the supreme expression of the power of God working to accomplish the reconciliation of the world unto himself. What the community of Christian faith apprehends in this man called Jesus of Nazareth is True Man, is one who was True Man because he was (in Dietrich Bonhoeffer's phrase) "the man for others" [22] *par excellence*. Here was a human life "totally pledged in responsibility for others, a life indeed so concentrated in the selflessness of its concern for all other life that it had the consequence of disclosing to the community of faith the tremendous fact that in his life the essential structure of all life had been revealed." [23] Here, in short, was a life so transparent to the ultimate depth and ground of our being as to compel the conclusion of the Roman centurion that "truly this man was the Son of God" (Mark 15:39); and the consistent witness of the New Testament is that what he is, God is too, so that to have seen the Man from Galilee is to have seen the Father (John 14:9), is to have beheld the Father's glory (the name of which is Love).

But, of course, what is bitterest in the deep mystery of human life is that such holiness as was incarnate in the life of this man can manifest itself redemptively in a sinful world only at the cost of suffering on the part of him who is the bearer of it. Yet, though the True Man was bound to be the victim of other men, he did also finally disclose himself to be their great High Priest as well. For so completely did he identify himself with what is marred and broken in human life and so fully did he consent to be bruised by the chastisement of others' woes—so absolutely was he "the man for others"—that the community of faith was convinced that in his great heart there was strength and compassion sufficient to bear all the discredit and reproach of our sin. And thus not only the apostolic people but all their descendants across the years have been unanimous in their faith that Christ is "our Passover" (I Cor. 5:7), a paschal lamb slain as a "sin-offering," as the "full, perfect, and sufficient sacrifice, oblation, and satisfaction, for the sins of the whole world." Surely, Christians universally have felt that the broken body and the spilled blood of the Man called Christ have established and sealed a New Covenant for our peace: so, being reassured by his having stood in our place and pleading nothing of our own but only his Passion, we pray, in the language of William Bright's old hymn:

> Look, Father, look on his anointed face
> And only look on us as found in him.
> Look not on our misusings of thy grace,
> Our prayer so languid, and our faith so dim.
> For, lo, between our sins and their reward
> We set the Passion of thy Son, our Lord.

It needs to be stressed, however, that, in Christian soteriology, the Immolated One who is wounded for our transgressions and whose "expiation" of our sin makes the "full, perfect, and sufficient" atoning sacrifice is not an unlucky martyr, picked out of the human community at random as one chosen to be a kind of scapegoat for the "satisfaction" of an irascible Tyrant in the Courts of Heaven. This is doubtless sometimes suggested by the traditional imagery of blood-sacrifice and the notions of penal substitution often prominent in popular religion. But nothing could be further from the truth. For in the Church's confession, Jesus of Nazareth is "very God of very God" and "of one substance with the Father": in the technical language of Trinitarian theology, he is the second "hypostasis" or "person" of the triune Godhead—which means that, from first to last, the provision that is made for "man's 'homecoming' to God" [24] is made by none other than God himself, for he who offered his body for our redemption was the very Son of God, indeed the Lamb slain from the foundation of the world.

Christian theology, however, has always been careful to maintain—and with especial emphasis since the Reformation—that our "justification" through the atoning work of Christ becomes truly efficacious only when it is accepted in faith. Though the True Man was interceding for us on Calvary and was offering to God not only himself but mankind as well, we are "enabled to join with Him in the eternal, once-for-all, offering He made and makes on our behalf" [25] only when we take hold of his atonement in an act of radical trust. The doctrine of justification by faith means that *the* representative man, in being perfectly obedient to the Heavenly Father and in thus providing a definitive disclosure of what it means to be truly human, has given us a new kind of access to the righteousness to which we are called of God. For not only was Christ a ransom for the many, enabling us in our unrighteousness to be accepted as though we were righteous: he did also, by establishing the fact of our acceptability, make it possible for us to accept ourselves—so that henceforth, knowing that we *are* accepted despite our unacceptability, we are liberated from all the old necessities to accredit ourselves both to ourselves and to others. And not only are we, as it were, liberated *into* acceptance of ourselves, but we are also now freed *to* acceptance of others: as Paul Tillich says, "We experience the grace of being able to accept the life of another, even if it be hostile and harmful to us, for, through grace, we know that it belongs to the same Ground to which we belong, and by which we have been accepted." [26]

The only requirement is that these new possibilities of reconciliation be accepted in "faith," that there be in a truly deep and living way a subjective appropriation of what the New Man has achieved. But it is important to see—along the lines so sensitively sketched out by Rudolf Bultmann— that the *decision to believe* is a thing profoundly different from the other decisions of life. For, normally, as Bultmann says, we come to a decision about this or that "on the basis of considerations which remain outside the sphere of the decision," [27] and, once the decision is made, we stand, as we say, behind it and are prepared to back it up. Nor are we changed ourselves by the normal decisions of our lives: instead, it is the external circumstances of our lives which in one way or another are altered. But, in the decision for faith, "all the considerations which otherwise have a motivating power for a man [are] uprooted . . . and are called in question," "so that man . . . stands, as it were, in the open"; and it is in this moment, when all security is abandoned, that faith is constituted, coming to pass in such a way that "man cannot understand [it] . . . as an established work of his own purposeful activity, but simply as a God-given free act," [28] as a gift of the Holy Spirit.

But, of course, the "justification" that is accepted in "faith" does not erase man's sinfulness. Instead, the situation of every believer is precisely that which St. Paul describes as his own: "Not as though I had already attained, either were already perfect: but I follow after, if that I may apprehend that for which also I am apprehended of Christ Jesus. Brethren, I count not myself to have apprehended: but this one thing I do, forgetting those things which are behind, and reaching forth unto those things which are before, I press toward the mark for the prize of the high calling of God in Christ Jesus" (Phil. 3:12-14). What we are given, in other words, through the reconciling work of Christ is a new courage to face ourselves; and we are also given a new *easiness* in our relations with others: we are no longer harried and driven by what Bultmann calls "the urge for recognition," [29] for now we know ourselves to *be* recognized, so that there is no great need to "prove" ourselves and thus to make the anxious self, with its hunger for security, the organizing center of life. But, though justification by faith gives us a new freedom to face ourselves and others and our human future, we are not thereby suddenly made wholly righteous and free of sin. We have, to be sure, been "apprehended of Christ," but, as we press on toward the prize of our high calling, there is a steady deepening in our awareness that we have only the first fruits of the Spirit, that there is never any escaping the "either/or" in the concrete situations of life, and that there are heights of true holiness that always remain to be scaled. "Sanctification" is the name that Christian tradition gives to this process of growth and advance, under the tutelage of the Holy Spirit.

Having affirmed that man is created in the image of God but that he has "fallen" into alienation from God and does therefore require, in order to be put right, such a radical provision as God makes by way of Jesus and his cross—having affirmed these things, Christian anthropology has it as its final concern to tell us who the Christian man is. And, here, perhaps the best point at which to begin is with a classic formulation by St. Paul, who suggests that he who chooses to be with Christ and "in" Christ is one who is "always bearing about in the body the dying of the Lord Jesus, that the life also of Jesus might be made manifest in [his] . . . body" (II Cor. 4:10). This is to say that the Christian man is not one for whom the great sacrifice of Calvary is merely one event among other events which, from time to time, produces mental and emotional reactions of various kinds, and which is to be chronicled by historians of the first century A.D.: the Christian man is, rather, the man for whom the event of Calvary has entered, in a profoundly ontological way, into the living present that he inhabits, having become the very shape and pattern of his own daily existence. He is indeed the man who has so united himself "with the great act of God's love in Christ" that our Lord is enabled to "reproduce Himself, His life, His free offering," [30] in the manhood of *this* disciple. He is the man who (in paraphrase of the Supplication in the Consecration Prayer of the Anglican rite) offers and presents himself unto God, his soul and body, "to be a reasonable, holy, and living sacrifice." So he is a priest, for that is what priesthood is all about—namely, the offering of sacrifices, of gifts, to God. The essential actions in the life of the Christian man are, we may even say, the basic priestly actions that are performed by Christ our Brother, for, like the great High Priest, the true disciple (a) takes his life, and (b) breaks it, and (c) gives it to his neighbor for bread.

Yet this "reasonable, holy, and living sacrifice" of the Christian man is not merely an expression of "individual priesthood," for if "priesthood [is] to reach its goal, it must be representative." [31] And the priesthood of the Christian man is the priesthood of the *laos,* of the assembly of those who are summoned by God to "show forth the praises of

Him who hath called you out of darkness into His marvellous light" (I Pet. 2:9). The *diakonia*, the ministry, that is borne by the Christian man is, in other words, a ministry that is his by reason of his membership in the new community among men which is the consequence of Christ's work of reconciliation. And thus we are brought to what may be regarded as the fourth principle of Christian anthropology, that the Christian man is man-in-the-Church.* And since *the* Catholic action of the Church is the Eucharist—which makes the necessary bridge between the "dying of the Lord Jesus" and the "living sacrifice" of the disciple in his own moment of history—we may say with Dom Gregory Dix:

> Over against the dissatisfied "Acquisitive Man" and his no less avid successor the dehumanised "Mass-Man" of our economically focussed societies . . . Christianity sets the type of "Eucharistic Man"—man giving thanks with the product of his labours upon the gifts of God, and daily rejoicing with his fellows in the worshipping society which is grounded in eternity.[32]

There is, in other words, in the discipleship under the Lord Jesus Christ not only a certain "cost" (as Bonhoeffer says[33]) of labor and suffering, but also in the "crossed" life a very great joy—and man, in the high drama of the Christian pilgrimage, is not only *"trailing* clouds of glory" but also living *in* glory, one who is given the Morning Star[34] and "to whom it was promised on the night before Calvary that he should henceforth eat and drink at the table of God and be a king." [35]

---

* For the phrase "man-in-the-Church" I am indebted to the Protestant writer William Hamilton, who uses it pejoratively, to set what he takes to be its "Catholic" connotation over against what are for him more congenial "Protestant" conceptions of the Christian life. See his interesting book, *The New Essence of Christianity* (New York: Association Press, 1961), especially, pp. 104-105.

The proposition that the Christian man is man-in-the-Church is surely a very hard kind of saying. It will seem to many to imply an arrogant prescription of the range beyond which the Holy Spirit is inoperative. And, were any such prescription to be attempted, it would be a most intolerable form of arrogance indeed. For the Spirit of God is universally operative: it "bloweth where it listeth, and thou . . . canst not tell whence it cometh, and whither it goeth" (John 3:8). As Charles Péguy reminds us, "Grace is insidious, it twists and is full of surprises. . . . When it doesn't come from the right, it comes from the left. . . . When it doesn't come from above, it comes from below; and when it doesn't come from the center it comes from the circumference." [36] In the secular reformer's passion for social justice, in the unbaptized artist's stringent exploration of vast tracts of uncharted terrain in human experience, in the agnostic scientist's rigorous search for the basic laws and structures of natural reality, and in countless other fields of social and cultural endeavor, we must be careful not to be so unimaginative as to fail to discern the activity of the Spirit. And we must even be prepared to keep a lively sense of the probability that, in many of the critical areas of contemporary life, the Royal Priesthood of the Faithful will in fact find its fulfillment *through* all sorts of creative personalities and movements outside the Church, for the assembly of the people of God is today often a people of the *diaspora,* in many ways scattered and, through tragic misunderstandings, separated from one another. Nevertheless, since the Church is that community of men who live consciously under the cross and who do consciously witness to the providential prevenience of God's grace, we may say that the Spirit is, pre-eminently, operative in and through the Church and that the Christian man is, *normally,* man-in-the-Church.

There is still another ground, of course, from which an objection may be taken to this formulation of things. For to say that the Christian man is man-in-the-Church will imply to some that the Christian's commitment is to a special department of experience and activity—the ecclesiastical, the churchly—which is over against or at least separable from "the world": and it will quickly be concluded that such a view of the Christian's place, as something over against "the world," does in fact commit him to a ghetto in which he can hardly be expected to have any real chance of carrying out the vocation laid upon him by Christ, of being "for others" and of living what Bonhoeffer called the life of "deputyship." [37] But surely such a conclusion can be drawn only on the basis of a profound misunderstanding of what the Church in fact really is: for, in the very moment in which it becomes a "religious society" turned inward on the special precincts of a life which it believes itself to have independently of its commitment to the world, in that moment it ceases to be the Church of God; and it does so because the primary concern of the true *ekklesia* is for *leitourgia,* for service, and it is turned not inward but outward and earthward, toward everything in human life that is problematic and broken and in need of restoration to sanity and peace. As Bonhoeffer says:

. . . the Church of Jesus Christ is the place, in other words the space in the world, at which the reign of Jesus Christ over the whole world is evidenced and proclaimed. This space of the Church, then, is not something which exists on its own account. It is from the outset something which reaches out far beyond itself, for indeed it is not the space of some kind of cultural association such as would have to fight for its own survival in the world, but it is the place where testimony is given to the foundation of all reality in Jesus Christ. The Church is the place where testimony and serious thought are given to God's reconciliation of the world with Himself in Christ, to His having so loved the world that He gave His Son for its sake. The space of the Church is not there in order to try to deprive the world of a piece of its territory, but precisely in order to prove to the world that it is still the world, the world which is loved by God and reconciled with Him. The Church has neither the wish nor the obligation to extend her space to cover the space of the world. She asks for no more space than she needs for the purpose of serving the world by bearing witness to Jesus Christ and to the reconciliation of the world with God through Him. The only way in which the Church can defend her own territory is by fighting not for it but for the salvation of the world. . . . And so the first demand which is made of those who belong to God's Church is not that they should be something in themselves, not that they should, for example, set up some religious organization . . . but that they shall be witnesses to Jesus Christ before the world.[38]

So the fact that the "knight of faith" is man-in-the-Church does not at all mean that he stands in opposition to the *saeculum.* For to be in-the-Church is not to be in any other world than that which is inhabited by all men; nor is it to be in a community whose mission it is to administer the predominance of the *regnum gratiae* over the *regnum naturae* or to bully the world into acceding to some special *Weltanschauung:* it is, rather, simply to be in the community which, having encountered the essential truth about human existence in Jesus Christ, wants to release into the whole of life the healing influence of his *agape.* So the sphere of the Christian man's obedience is none other than the world itself, and he does not spend his time in commuting between "two Cities," for there is no other place to go to beside or above this teeming human City in which we are born and in which we live and work and die. And there is no other place to which he should want to go, since it was with this world that

Christ himself made one, so identifying himself with it and
so absorbing into himself "the poisons by which it had been
defaced that He became the author and head" [39] of New
Being, of a world "endowed again with the limitless possibilities of the original creation—even at those points or in
those areas where it still *looks* most forlorn." [40] And thus it is
for this reason, says Alec Vidler, that

. . . the mystical Body of Christ, the community of his Holy
Spirit, the Church, rightly seeks to identify itself with the whole
life of the world and to serve it—instead of standing aloof or
apart. The true Church refuses to respond to the puritan or
sectarian admonition to come out of the accursed city and be a
community as separate as possible from the world.[41]

Indeed, in Vidler's striking phrase, the Christian man's vocation is to a "holy worldliness." [42]

So now we have come full circle: created in the "image of
God"; "fallen"; restored to God by Christ's reconciling work,
for life in the Blessed Community of *diakonia*, of "deputyship," of service "for others"—this, in short, is the story that
Christianity tells about humankind. And though it is a
story that on one ground or another may be rejected by a
generation eager to congratulate itself on having arrived at
the threshold of what is trippingly spoken of in the Sunday
supplements as our "post-Christian" age, there is at least one
ground on which it is gloriously secure against all attack.
For, amidst all the isms and ologies of our time which willy-
nilly have worked to impugn or to reduce the fullness of
man's human stature, at least it cannot be said of the Christian faith that it is in any way *against* man. It wants light for
those who "sit in darkness, and in the shadow of death," as
we are reminded in the *Benedictus* of the Morning Office; it
does not ask man to fling himself out of this world into the

arms of a timeless eternity. It asks him, rather, to move more deeply into this world; it asks him not to reject himself with a shudder of fastidious disgust at his creatural limitations but to return to himself, to his true human stature, and to "be joyful in the Lord." And then, it says—and then, "All things are yours."

2

Post-Renaissance Man

by Ronald Gregor Smith

Teach us to care and not to care
Teach us to sit still.

> T. S. ELIOT, *Ash-Wednesday*

"Who am I?" asked Dietrich Bonhoeffer in one of his most moving poems, written in a Nazi prison.[1] And like many of the Psalms, which take in the whole world in their course, he too ends with words of commitment:

> Whoever I am, you know me, I am yours, O God.

Between the question and the answer lies man in his world. Bonhoeffer's view of the world has become the subject of many studies. It contains immensely fruitful insights and ambiguities, but is on the whole too fragmentary and casual to be used in any systematic way.

Certainly it is the ambiguities which are the most immediately striking thing about the modern view of man and his world. In the words of Max Scheler:

> In no other period of human knowledge has man ever become more problematic to himself than in our own day. We have a scientific, a philosophical and a theological anthropology that know nothing of each other. Therefore we no longer possess any clear and consistent idea of man. The ever-growing multiplicity

31

of the particular sciences that are engaged in the study of man
has much more confused and obscured than elucidated our concept of man.[2]

It is the purpose of this essay to elucidate from a theological
point of view the concept of man which has arisen since the
Renaissance. Although the point of view is theological, it is
not intended to be dogmatic in the pejorative sense of a positivist, heteronomous theology which wishes to impose either
some specific metaphysic or a set of propositions that claim
authority as revealed truth. But we take our starting point
from the very ambiguities of the empirical, historical situation.

How may we describe the present situation? Man is his
own master, and thus aware that there are no bounds to his
powers. He can do anything that he wishes to do. At the
same time he is without hope. He plans to reach the moon,
but he is desperately afraid that he will not have the time to
do so.[3] He is free, and come of age, but he is also a slave of
ideologies. He recognizes that his existence as a man carries
with it the demand to be himself, as a single personal being
(in Kierkegaard's phrase), and at the same time he finds himself continually threatened with immersion in the life of
the collective—and he even desires this, in order that he
may evade the hard demand to be a single person.

There is a fearful ambivalence here, and the man of today
does not know where to turn. No analysis, from whatever
perspective, is satisfactory which ignores this; and even if the
attempt is made (as in this essay) to trace a dominant motif
and possibility for man, no static harmonizing of the con-
traries can be expected: the ambivalence can never be removed. The risk for man remains: his very nature is a risk,
and the issue is unpredictable.

Man's understanding of himself today is weighted by the

historical decisions which he has inherited. All history is man's struggle to understand himself. But even his awareness of those decisions today is both limited and confused, so that he appears to himself now as the master, now as the slave; now as the mature and deliberate manipulator of nature and history, and now as a mere faceless number in the machinery of productivity; now as full of *Angst,* and now as an undifferentiated addition to the congealed mass of a static and meaningless agglomeration of being.

The resolution of this confusion—but not of the inherent ambivalence—depends on man's own decision. He is what he decides to be. This decision in turn depends on his understanding of his historical existence. Whether he chooses the "holy hypochondria" [4] of his heterogeneity, and the endless restless movement of his spirit which is its expression, or whether he sinks into homogeneity, like a sick man unwilling to get better and to brave the world again, will be determined by himself and by no extraneous powers. Samuel Beckett is right to place his characters simply in the situation of waiting;[5] even waiting without hope, "for hope would be hope for the wrong thing." [6] But there is a hope beyond hope of things and powers, and Beckett has scarcely done more than approach the threshold of this other dimension of hope. It is a historical hope, and it is with this that we are concerned here.

It is again Bonhoeffer who provides the impetus for man's understanding of himself in history. He speaks of man's autonomy, especially in relation to his "discovery of the laws by which the world lives and manages in science, social and political affairs, art, ethics and religion"; and while he does not wish to get involved in a discussion of the exact date of this new phenomenon, he speaks of a time "about the thirteenth century." [7]

It is clear that, whatever the qualifications we have to add
to such an observation, there was in fact a remarkable
efflorescence of man's activity which we may fairly place as
succeeding the Middle Ages.[8] It included the liberation from
the metaphysic of the Middle Ages, and from the standpoint
of the present day may be described as the first manifestations
of what we now call secularism.[9] I take this at present, without prejudice to a fuller definition, to mean a predominantly
"this-worldly" standpoint. In its positive expression it has
been characterized by Dilthey as the development of "free
manifoldness," that is, the spread of a deliberate and conscious autonomy and individualizing of the interests and enterprises, both "purely" intellectual and then more and more
technological, of Renaissance and post-Renaissance man.[10]
For the interest of our analysis we may note that the negative expression of this development is that modern secularist
man is more and more ready to manage his life without
reference to God.

But this is no more than a provisional description. It is
precisely in the ambiguities of this secularism, and especially
in the meaning in this context of the word "God," that we
have to look for clues for a right decision. Even on the basis
of what has already been said here about the empirical condition of man today, it should be clear that there is an uncertainty, even a malaise, in the heart of "secularism." It is
an interesting indication of this that several writers have attempted recently to distinguish between a necessary "secularity" and a decadent or sterile "secularism." [11]

To grasp the full implications of what happened to man's
self-understanding at the Renaissance, however, and to understand, so far as understanding is possible, why such a
change took place then, it is necessary to look further back
into the story of European man than Bonhoeffer suggested.

It is certainly upon the recognition by Renaissance man of his own responsibility for his history that the whole issue turns. There was undoubtedly a novel, vivid, and creative recognition of man's freedom: no external forces, no arbitrary fate, but man himself in his deliberate assumption of responsibility for his own history was seen, sometimes with melancholy but more characteristically with exhilaration and even with pride, as "the free creator of his destiny." [12] The life of Pico della Mirandola (1463-94) is perhaps the most fascinating illustration of this audacious enterprise. It was his ambition to unite the whole of European thought in a single view of man. Though his attempt was never completed, so that we are left with little more than a legend, nevertheless in the writings he has left, he is to be understood as more than an eclectic philosopher. He wanted to bring Moses and Plato, the Cabala, and even the Schoolmen into subservience to Christ. His discourse *On the Dignity of Man,* intended as an introduction to the nine hundred theses with which he challenged the Church and the whole society of the learned, is more than an exercise in the glorification of man and his powers. It is the prelude to a new understanding of human history. His ideas, it is true, struck no roots at the time, and they cannot be pursued in detail here. What is of interest for our purpose, however, is that Pico, as one of the great characteristic figures of the Italian Renaissance, saw the move forward in terms of a new understanding of the past, and basically indeed in terms of a new understanding of Christ. The hope he had for man's future was thus derived from the hope he found in an event of the past.

We must keep this paradox in mind as we take this hint from Pico to look back into our history. And if we restrict what it is practicable to say here to the nature of biblical faith, this is nevertheless not intended as a restriction to any

dogmatic inheritance. Rather, we wish to lengthen and en-
rich the perspective from which we may better assess the
powers that were stirring at the Renaissance.

My basic contention can be stated briefly. The original
impulse for the Renaissance and thus for the modern view
of man comes from the biblical faith. The secularism of our
time has its sanction in the prophetic faith. And Christ is
the unreserved, unconfused, and completely consistent secularist of history. It is only on the basis of the biblical view
of faith, of man and God, and in the clearest expression of
this view, namely, in the life of Christ, that a real understanding and thus a radical critique of modern secularist
man can be achieved.

Now clearly both the Old Testament and the New Testament are a rich quarry for theologians and for students of
religious phenomena. But the biblical faith itself is in the
first instance neither theology nor religion. It is primarily
history, seen simultaneously as man's actions and God's
actions, but not separable from one another in their actuality. Indeed, the interaction is so complete that from the standpoint of biblical faith we may say that history is seen both as
man's history and as God's history. It is the historicity of God
which is the inescapable basis of the biblical view of man;
and it is the historicity of man which is the only way in
which God may be believed.

What the Bible provides is not theology in the sense of
speculation about God. There is certainly a wealth of reflection about God, but it arises out of the context of historical action. Thus there is no questioning of the existence of
God, and no effort to catalogue his attributes. The Bible is
interested neither in the question whether God exists nor
in the question what God is in himself. It recounts the engagement of God with men in their own history. In so doing

it witnesses to the historicity of God. When the Psalmist's enemies ask him, "Where is your God?" * he has no discursive argument ready to persuade them. He can only point to his faith in the movement of God in many different ways in history. What the men of the Bible bear witness to may be described as God's "coming to speech." And this "speaking" consistently takes place within a situation of extreme personal engagement. The "revelation" is not an objective account, nor an overwhelming theophany, nor a mythological structure. It is no more and no less than a demand laid upon a man, or a people, in and through the actual historical possibilities of the time, for which the response of faith or rejection is required in an unqualified way. What biblical faith does *not* assert is of the utmost significance.

That God does not have a being in analogy with our being, that the Word is not a mystical experience, that faith is not an experience or any human capacity, that God cannot be conceived as a substance, nor his work as causality, and that the holy history cannot be understood as a process—all these burning and heavy-laden negations are given with the basic structure of the Bible.[13]

These negations clear the air of the Bible. Indeed, they clear the world of gods and powers. They even leave God himself out of the world. But this does not mean that the world is abandoned or that the recognition of God in history, of the historicity of God, must be annulled. On the contrary, it is only in the paradoxical recognition of God's absence from the world that the world is freed to become what it can become, and what God wishes it to be. Only in a world which is completely dedivinized in this way is any advent of

---

* E.g. Ps. 42:3: "My tears have been my food day and night, while men say to me continually, 'Where is your God?' "

God possible. The presence of God is dialectically conjoined with his absence. In the biblical view man must learn to live *etsi deus non daretur,* as though God were not given. God not as a bit of the world, God not as an extension of the world or of man's thought about the world, God not as a monstrous imposition upon the world, but God given to the world as though he were not given—this is the rich and paradoxical summary of the biblical faith in God.

Certainly, it is this God who is "completely other" than his people who nevertheless is with and for his people, and gives meaning to their whole history. But in the biblical faith there is no question of the reflective establishment of a doctrine either of God's transcendence or of his immanence. It is even misleading to say that in the Bible we find the definitive theological assertion of monotheism. Of course it is true that reflections of the discursive understanding may arise on the basis of the biblical records; but they are reflections after the event. And the event itself is different: it is always *in actu,* in action, in the actual situation of the man who is called upon, required, to face his own history in terms of a present demand upon him for faith.

And what the Bible provides is not religion either, in the sense of man's search for God, and the manipulation of powers in order to reach him. Not even man's most splendid achievements can reach God or touch him. Indeed, from the spectator's point of view the most obvious thing about the story of ancient Israel is the monotony of failure in their highest ambitions and enterprises. Yet the significance, even in the failure, is that Israel recognized that their God was nevertheless with them and for them. This is not to be understood in terms of a theodicy, as though God were apportioning the fit reward, or punishment, according to the nature of the achievement or the failure. For the people lived in and with the faith that God was active in their history. This was simply how things were: they did not need to search for God, because he was already there, and had found them. But at the same time there was no safety in this conviction, no guarantee for their historical existence. The only assurance was in their conviction: it was *certitudo,* not *securitas;* they were utterly convinced, and at the same time launched on an unpredictable course.

It is therefore also misleading to try to isolate the element of the "numinous" from the life of faith as the characteristic element. There is no isolation of any religious element, however described, in the history of Israel. Even if the encounter with God in history brings with it the fear of the Lord, this cannot be interpreted as the experience of a "frisson" of the "otherworldly," far less of the "uncanny." For example, when Isaiah encounters the presence of the Lord in the temple, what we are faced with in the account is the integral connection of Isaiah's call with his historical task: "Here am I, send me," is his response, and with these words he is launched upon a sober, even matter-of-fact, mission.

In the New Testament all these elements—the historicity, the conjunction of the presence and the absence of God, the pretheological and the suprareligious concern—are to be found once more. But now the issue of Israel's history has narrowed down to an almost intolerable point of tension and paradox. The tension reaches its climax in the failure of the mission of Jesus, the paradox in its vindication. Here the man of faith takes the center of the stage, and alone. Here the historical responsibility is at its purest and most crucial. And nothing helps, nothing in the best efforts of religion. Jesus came into the world to destroy religion, says Paul Tillich in effect[14]; and the powers of the world and the efforts of man to establish a means of solving the riddle of man's being and destiny are at this point shown up as fruitless. But Tillich's dictum needs to be modified. For the efforts of men are not simply destroyed, to leave no hope. They are conquered. In other words, even in the crucial moment of the cry of dereliction from the cross, "My God, my God, why hast thou forsaken me?" Jesus is not simply alone. The very invocation of God implies the recognition of God's concern. Here the world is finally and conclusively emptied of hope, and cleared of would-be powers. And in this clearance the reality of the "nevertheless" of faith comes into its own. The story of Israel reaches in the crucifixion of Jesus the point where the world is definitively released from all the powers of the world, where man is faced, in the person of Jesus, with the last decision about himself and his destiny, and is left all alone—in face of God.

This may be described as the story of man's religious yearnings or of his theological inquiries only in the sense that he is brought up short against their inadequacy. And here he is faced, with a unique concentration of purity and force, with the old question of what he is.

The question addressed to man at this point must not be reduced to a matter of mythological apprehensions or theological propositions about the nature of Christ. We must understand the question as carrying with it the claim that here we encounter the last Word of God. But how are we to understand this *eschaton,* this lastness, in relation to our ongoing history and especially to our normal view of religion, and to our immense modern confusion about what man really is?

An answer to this question is implicit in what has been said about biblical faith. But it is not self-evident or easy. The difficulty does not lie so much in the superficial obstacles—for example, the divided voice of the Church, or the unsurprising ambiguities of hypocrisy and self-complacency and self-righteousness and narrow-mindedness which are the constant temptations of professing Christians. For anyone who is asking with true concern what he thinks he ought to be, and how he understands the enigma of his own existence, will not be unduly influenced by the sight of the professing Christian yielding to his temptations. For he will also notice, with astonishment perhaps, the equal persistence of the man who professes to live by faith. And if he has any inkling of the nature of this faith, he will not ask for the removal of this ambiguity, but for the reason why, in spite of it, such persistence is possible at all.

From this brief look at the historical course of biblical faith we have seen that it is in the overcoming of religion, the reduction of all other gods in the world to silence, and in the concentrated pressure upon history of the God who is both absent and present, that the possibility was established for man to go his own way in a liberated world. But this possibility has never been more than dimly recognized, let alone realized. So today we are the heirs not only of this possibility in principle, but also of a confusion of images of man. We have now, in conclusion, to attempt a separation of images. The confusion might be briefly and comprehensively described as due to the failure of the Renaissance secularist insight to be worked out in a radical dialectic with the image of the new man in Christ, and in a radical conflict with the remnant images in man's consciousness.

I suggest that we may see altogether four images of what man is today. While these images are separable and distinct, they are all at home in more or less strength within each one of us.

The first image is Adam. In the mythology of the Old Testament, Adam is the first man. What sort of man? Is he good or bad? Is he what he can be simply in the sense of be-

coming more and more what he is? Or is there an "ought" in
his existence which implies a break, a discontinuity, a double
nature?

Adam is clearly recognized as related to God; but just as
clearly he is seen as out of relation to God. He is historical
man; that is, after the mythological account of the Fall has
been described, he is seen as the man we still know today—
broken, in a state of unrest, tension, and misery. But at the
same time, the grandeur of his origin is not denied, and the
grandeur of his possibilities is still present to him, providing
him indeed with nourishment for his unrest and misery. At
the same time, no return is possible. History is seen as irreversible; and after he is driven from the Garden of Eden,
from his state of "dreaming innocence," man is launched on
the course of the same history, as we may clearly recognize
by looking into our own selves. The familiarity of the mythology should not blind us to the penetrating power of the
analysis. We are all this Adam, and we are all heirs simultaneously of his grandeur and his misery:

> The whole earth is our hospital
> Endowed by the ruined millionaire,
> Wherein, if we do well, we shall
> Die of the absolute paternal care
> That will not leave us, but prevents us everywhere.[15]

But the answer to which T. S. Eliot has already alluded in
these lines, by speaking of the incessant "paternal care" which
is to cure us by a death of the sickness of Adam, is not a matter of course. Are we to interpret the cure as being a matter
of religion? The image of *Homo religiosus,* religious man, is
the second of the images that in some form is discernible in
us all. This has indeed traditionally been the favorite image
for man when he is driven to despair in the Adam he finds in

himself. And it is still very much alive in modern man, as it was alive in the time of the Renaissance. Even if we agree with Bonhoeffer that the age of religion is past, it is only in a limited sense that this is true. The age which accepted man's destiny as being determined within a metaphysical frame of the natural and the supernatural, with his salvation assured by his proper adherence to an authority of grace regarded as seizing him with arbitrary power—that age is certainly past. So too is the age of individualist religion and piety, whatever the rearguard actions which may be fought on behalf of what is a peculiarly Protestant heterodoxy.

But if we understand religion in the sense of the Bible—in the sense, that is, to which the biblical faith is so consistently hostile—and more generally as we see it at work in the nonbiblical religions, as the means of building up the powers of man in order to establish with God a relation which is already potentially present in man—in a religious *a priori* or a basic identity of man's being with God, or the like—then this type of religion is by no means past. It may be found within the styles of life and worship encouraged by the churches, but it may also be seen outside official Christianity. Certainly, it takes very different and varied forms outside the life of the churches, and the name of God has mostly been suppressed. This silence about God, however, is a more honest indication of this kind of religiousness than is the calling upon his name at the wrong address. But whether this form of religion is officially within the churches, or whether it is outside, in the form of adherence to some ideology, the basic feature is the same: it is the worship of some bit of the world, masquerading as absolute, and it does not matter whether this takes the form of some "secularist" faith (such as certain brands of so-called scientific humanism, or nationalism, or aestheticism, or moralism) or of one of the current variations of Christianity. What we are faced with, in each instance, is the basic characteristic of the second image, namely, the build-up of assurances within the world in order to secure man from the icy blast of the still unanswered question: Who then am I? The image of the religious man, however attractive at times to us all, and whether it is expressed in the styles of modern scientism or in the old-fashioned forms of dogmatic Christianity, is unable to penetrate beyond the world of objects.

Religion can indeed take many forms. Thus even modern secularism can illustrate the persistence and the ubiquity of the religious short-circuiting of the question of man. The greatest problem which faces the candid secularist today, who has learned something of the lesson of the Renaissance, is how he is to avoid ending in the prison of his own self. If it is true that the religious man (as distinct from the man of faith) simply makes a detour over symbols that pretend to aim at God, and returns to his own self,[16] so too the secular man of today, while he may avoid the particular pretense of turning to God, nevertheless returns only too easily to himself. He wanders in a no-man's land in which No-man, Nemo, is the only reflection he sees when he looks within himself or outside himself. The terror of an infinite regress of mirrors is the nightmare of modern secularist man's self-exploration. So he tries to justify his self-understanding by abstractions about the future of man, or the preservation of civilization, or happiness, or even by asserting the virtue of innovation for its own sake. This secularist man, who is the third image of man in all of us today, in more or less clarity of outline, desires to have an eschatology which is like Melchizedek in the Bible, without any genealogy, suddenly appearing on the scene of history, without beginning and without end. This can only mean that secularist man of this type, when this particular image gains the ascendancy in his life, is turned in on himself in the most calamitous self-despair or in an even more ominous self-esteem. The religion associated with the old Gnostic mythology regarded this world as a prison from which the soul longed to be released. But the unradical secularism of our time desires to make a virtue out of what appears to it to be the necessity of man's complete and absolute imprisonment in his own self.

But to choose oneself in this way means the negation of man's real dialectic with his own history. It is not basic liberation, but basic slavery. It is, incidentally, an abrogation of the historical concern which is so splendidly exemplified at the Renaissance.

The historical hope, which is the motif of this analysis, lies in the fourth image. By this I mean the biblical image which is adumbrated in the prophetic faith and present to faith in the person, or the event, of Christ. He is, as St. Paul says, "the last Adam" or "the second man" (I Cor. 15:45, 47). He is, to faith, the new historical possibility of man; he is the invitation to man, supplying both the question and the possibility of the answer regarding what man is. He is, to faith, what man can be, and what God wants man to be. He is man's history and God's history in one.

This is not the place for a survey of the whole range of theological statements about Christ. What is important for our purpose is to recognize the power that is present in the open facing of the image of this man. To this end I restrict myself to a few observations.

First, the image of Christ as the "last" man, or as the eschatological event, does not imply that by historical research we may be able to construct a picture of Jesus, guaranteed authentic, and carrying with it as a self-evident "fact" of history the claim to present a static, ascertainable, and demonstrable truth about the ultimate nature of man. This kind of reconstruction, even if it were possible, would not be the living historical and eschatological event which is the heart of the Christian message, and the source of Christian faith. But it would be at best an archaistic image, outside the real dynamic of history.

Second, the image of Christ as the eschatological man is not to be understood as reposing in past history. What is available to us of this image by the attentive and expectant listening to what we may hear from the biblical accounts is not the wholeness of this image. For it comes to us in the broken and ambiguous forms of history, and of our own history. If the appeal of Christianity were to be isolated to the objectified and necessarily mythological picture which is available to us through the forms and structures of history, then Christianity would indeed long ago have succumbed to the legendary and superstitious trappings with which it has again and again been embellished. But the image is available in the form of a claim upon us in our present being, in our present historical situation.

But third, the image of Christ as the last and decisive event of man's history is not just an encouragement to each man who has faith, as a means of withstanding and of maintaining hope in his present situation. But it is also an opening up of the future. It is the constant reopening of the present, pointing to ever new possibilities. In this sense the image of Christ is never complete in the whole course of human history. It is always ahead of us, inviting us to newness. It is able to do this just because it is *the* paradoxical event of human history in which man is challenged, and given the means, to establish a radical critique of all the other images. This is the only image for man which gives up hope in any powers of the world, and at the same time points man back to his responsibility for himself and his world.

The movement of the spirit of man which is thus established in history may be seen highlighted in the Renaissance; but in contrast with the possibilities inherent in this image, the Renaissance is no more than a gleam in the dark.

It is in this perspective that the modified secularism which is characteristic of our time has to be judged as being not radical enough. Only a Christian secularity, to use Gabriel Vahanian's term, is radical enough. That is to say, only a view of man which is both absolutely free, and absolutely responsible, is able to confront the dizzy prospect of our time —not indeed with equanimity, but with a reasonable hope. For only the radicality of the hopelessness of man's condition, with the simultaneous radicality of the new hope which he is given, as these are to be encountered, conjoined, in the single image of Christ as the man who in his being finalizes the reality of God's historical care—only this twofold radicality is able to carry man through the deepgoing antinomies of his existence.

The ambiguities, however, cannot be removed. The incessant slide of man's freedom into bondage or into license, the despair which is the other side of his hope, the threat of *nihil* which rushes in on him from each side of the narrow way are a necessary part of his destiny.

In this sense the secondary images of the religious man and of the short-term secularist, as well as the image of Adam, will always be with him. So far as the image of "religious man" is concerned, we are not simply "justified" by the Last Man, but (as Luther saw so clearly) we also remain sinners.

And as far as the modified secularism of our time is concerned, we are never freed in the sense of being given our freedom as an absolute possession. For this could only confirm us in the despair of self-possession. And as far as the image of Adam is concerned, this must remain so long as we recognize our basic historical finitude and relativity. But in and through the recognition of these historical images, man is able to deal with them. He is able to do so if he recognizes simultaneously what is happening to him and what is possible to him in virtue of the other image. This other image, the image of Christ as the Last Man, then appears to him both as thoroughly historical and as of another order from the rest of his historical self-understanding. It is thoroughly historical in that it is grounded in a historical life which is engaged in a realistic conflict with all the other historical images of man. And it is of another order from these in that it is simultaneously given to man as the final movement of God into history. In being encouraged by the central force of the Christian tradition to hold fast to this dominant image, the man of faith, in the unrest of his faith, finds that he is being held fast. And if we call this paradoxical experience man's final struggle for self-understanding, and the nearest to fullness of self-understanding that is given to him in history, then it must also be clearly affirmed that this struggle, when carried to the utmost in the depths of a faith and a hope in man and his history that simply will not let go, turns out to involve a gift. We are given the chance, the choice, to choose ourselves in this way. But if we make this choice of faith, that is, in the context of confrontation by the last image of man, then we will find that in truth we have not chosen ourselves, but we have been chosen.

This is the basic liberation of man. But it is a liberation into and for history. So in the strength of this basic liberation the other historical images still have a place, but they no longer have ultimate power. Adam, the religious man, and the free but lost secularist of our time are always with us and in us; but they are in principle overcome.

3

Man—In Light of Social Science and Christian Faith

by James M. Gustafson

What one understands about man depends upon the particular light in which he is seen, or more precisely, upon what vocabulary and relationships one chooses as the framework for interpretation. In theology man is interpreted in his relationship to God the Creator and Sustainer, to Jesus Christ the Son, and to the presence of the Spirit in the Church and the world. The fact that man is seen in this relationship (the one in which is seen the *real* man, according to Karl Barth and other theologians) predisposes the writer to use language appropriate to it. Man is seen as creature of God; he is seen as fallen from a state of faith and trust in God; he is seen as sinner in relation to God and to other men; he is seen as responsible to God in all his words and deeds; he is seen as participating in new life in Christ; he is seen in Christian freedom. All of these things that can be said about man in relationship to God, however, obviously do not exhaust what can be said about man in other relationships.

The secular philosopher of ethics has another light to turn upon man, different from the theologian's. He asks about man's moral action: Is it determined by his sentiments and his emotions? Or is it determined by a fundamental moral law that is grounded in human nature? Does he decide what his conduct ought to be in relation to the prevailing moral consensus of his community? Or is his behavior basically determined by some fundamental drives for self-preservation that reside in his psycho-physical being? Can he perceive values in things? Or does he act according to some rules of conduct set up by society?

Theological language and the vocabulary of ethics by no means exhaust the ways we have to describe and interpret man. There is political language, psychological language, aesthetic language, and many other forms. In this chapter, with an opening confession of necessary oversimplification, we are concerned to see what man looks like in the light of social science. The task is appallingly broad, and justice cannot be done to refinements in viewpoints, and to competing forces at debate within the sciences that deal with social behavior. To make it manageable, three themes have been selected as fairly pervasive in the social sciences: (*a*) man is viewed genetically—that is, in terms of the causal processes, and thus there is an emphasis on the determination of his present state by past events; (*b*) man is viewed functionally —that is, in terms of a creature with needs that seek fulfillment in various ways in order to survive; (*c*) man is viewed as researchable—that is, he can be defined in terms measurable by contemporary social research procedures.

Throughout the exposition of these themes, certain contrasts will be drawn with theological and moral interpretations of man. This is done not to demonstrate the superiority of theology and ethics to give the picture of "real" man, but to indicate the differences in frame of reference, and thus in the characteristics that are accentuated in the portrait of man. Nor is the procedure of contrast used to demonstrate the greater adequacy of social science themes about man; they will always be inadequate taken in themselves for those who think of man in relation to God, and who think of man in relation to moral responsibility. Actually, however, most Christians have absorbed much of the fundamental vision of man that is embedded in studies of his social behavior without consciousness of discrepancies between that view and those provided in the Christian tradition. Most of us act as if social determination is the whole story of man. Finally, however, both our action and the views of social sciences need to be questioned in the light of our Christian confession.

Behavior Is Determined

One of the oldest arguments among Western views of man deals with the extent of man's freedom versus the extent of his determination by forces outside himself. This has been an issue in philosophy: at one extreme Spinoza seems to say that the only freedom man has is his acquiescence to necessity; in his acceptance of the fact that he is determined by other forces, he finds the measure of freedom that he has. In contrast, Kant, who was interested in preserving a strong sense of moral responsibility, asserted that the essential character of the human self was outside the realm of the effects of causal factors, and could exercise reason and free will to determine behavior. The issue of freedom and determinism also has a long history of theological debate. Finally is each man predestined? Or does he determine his own destiny? If he is predestined, are all the detailed decisions of life governed by God's power? Or is there a realm of responsibility for the exercise of free choice? This debate continues in theological discourse: Christian existentialists stress the capacity for a free response of faith and obedience to God, and thus the ability to shape life and events. Theologians who still desire to interpret the providence of the almighty God are forced to find qualified ways to deal with freedom.

The social scientists have not taken part in this debate in philosophical and theological terms. Indeed, they tend to eschew such language, and aver that they are concerned only with such generalizations about human behavior as can be developed from observation and from refined empirical evidences. But social scientists do belong to a community of scholars who seek to understand what now exists in the light of cause-and-effect analysis; they look at the self in an effort to find out what conditions, causal factors, relationships, and occasions are most important in shaping behavior. Thus there is in the social sciences a predisposition to think in "behavioristic" terms, that is, in terms of the determination of human selfhood and action by turning to the antecedents of the present experience. There is a tendency to view the present self particularly in relation to its past experiences, and in relation to other selves, cultures, and institutions that presently exert decisive influence on behavior.

In Freudian psychology this is clearly the case. In order to understand the present condition of a personality, whether a healthy or an unhealthy one, the interpreter turns to the early experiences of the child. It is assumed that the decisive factors in the shaping of behavior characteristics occurred in the relationships of son to mother, of father to daughter, of siblings to each other. It is also assumed in the orthodox forms of this view, that the human sexual drive is of unique significance in determining how a person thinks, and what a person does. Fascinating biographical interpretations have been made from this point of view: Erik Erikson's *Young Man Luther* deals with an important religious historical figure; Ernest Jones's *Hamlet and Oedipus* uses psychoanalytic language to understand two great characters in literature.[1]

The social psychologists have tended to think a different set of factors to be more important in the determination of behavior than do the orthodox Freudians. They look to the effects of belonging to certain social groups, such as an ethnic immigrant community or the "middle class." Cultural anthropologists among them look at what the "ethos" and values of a culture do to the development of personality. Some of the writing in this vein is done in the manner of grand theorizing; in others research is done with great precision of measurement and analysis.

One of the early formulators of the general view of social behaviorism was the Chicago philosopher-psychologist G. H. Mead, whose *Mind, Self, and Society*[2] remains a landmark of fundamental theory of a social view of selfhood. Mead sees the self coming into being in two general stages. First, the child organizes in his own experience and behavior the attitudes that others have expressed toward him and toward each other in their gestures, their speech, and their actions. Self-identity comes into being by virtue of the internalization of the meanings of expressions that occur in the primary social relationships. The second stage is that of absorbing not only individual attitudes, but social attitudes of groups to which one belongs. Particular groups—the family, the social class, the church, the peer group—are "generalized others" to which a particular person responds, and to which he conforms to some extent in the organization of his own behavior.

This view of Mead's assumes that there is always an "I" that cannot be totally explained on the basis of past experience, and continues to be the organizing center of all the influences exerted upon the self. But there is also a "me" that is the fundamental core of identity resulting from the accruing effects of social participation in various groups. Thus, the analytic procedures can be crudely stated: If you want to understand and explain a person you know, turn to the various groups to which he has belonged and continues to belong. You will find that what is identifiable about him is the result of these social relationships. In the less precise words of a contemporary of Mead's, Charles Horton Cooley, the self "mirrors" other selves and groups to which it is related. In distinction from Cooley, Mead stresses the organizing center, the thinking self, as a factor that brings all these past influences together into some integrated unity.

Most cultural anthropologists and sociologists operate in the same basic frame of reference. Ralph Linton developed a general viewpoint in his *Cultural Background of Personality* that states the case as accepted with variations by many anthropologists. To be sure, there are "innate factors" that are not culturally determined, by which one can understand some of the differences between persons who share a common culture, but personality is largely shaped by the people and things that form one's environment. "The behavior of the members of any society and the forms of most of the objects which they use are largely stereotyped and can be described in terms of culture patterns." [3] It is through these stereotypical culture patterns that personalities take shape. Thus, in the famous study *Patterns of Culture* by Ruth Benedict, one finds "Apollonian" traits of personality, stressing rationality, self-control, and the like, to be characteristic of such a tribe as the Zuni Indians of the Southwest United States, and "Dionysian" traits, stressing competitiveness, aggressiveness, violence, and the like to be characteristic of Indians in the Northwest. The patterns of culture developed in relation to cultural heritage, physical environment, and social conditions become internalized in the individual members of particular societies.

The grand generalizations of earlier writers have provided a viewpoint, and certainly give insight to the observer. But they have been qualified and carefully refined by contemporary research. The blanket statements have been transformed into verifiable evidence of statistical probabilities that allow for exceptions to the general case. A recent study in the sociology of religion illustrates some of the refining process. Gerhard Lenski, in a study of people in the Detroit, Michigan, area, demonstrates that religious affiliation is a significant factor in the determination of attitudes and behavior of people. But rather than make a point as general as "if a child is raised in a Catholic home and church, he will reflect the patterns of Catholicism in his behavior," Lenski suggests that the religious "variable" has to be seen as one among many: the racial, ethnic, social class, and other factors. On the basis of a refined research procedure, he seeks to indicate the strength of the religious-group determination by sorting it out in reference to other factors, and then provides a statistical probability that can be stated in "more likely" types of generalizations such as "the middle class was more likely than the working class to believe in the availability of opportunities for workingmen's sons and in the importance of ability." Or, "white Protestants were more inclined than others to believe that the sons of workingmen have good chances for advancement." [4] The basic thesis remains the same, however, namely, if you wish to understand a person's attitude toward work, look at the groups to which he belongs, and you are likely to find the decisive influences.

The interpretation of the self as conditioned, or determined, results from the kinds of questions that the social scientist asks: What factors seem to cause behavior? How is behavior to be understood in relation to its antecedents? Thus with these questions in view the analyst sees the continuities of human behavior, within one person's life, and between the action of a person and the characteristics of the group to which he belongs.

In contrast to these questions, others can be asked about the self, in different languages, with different intentions. The ethicist might ask: Given a self that is facing the present and the future, how does he decide to act? What does he do? He is not asking, "How did the self get this way?" but rather, "Where does it go from here?" The social scientist, with his generalizations about behavior, might venture to predict what a person or a group will do on the basis of their knowledge of the past. But the moralist, by virtue of being oriented to the present and future in his questions, stresses the unpredictabilities of selfhood, the possibilities for doing the novel, the creative thing.

The theologian might find the analysis of human behavior given from the viewpoint of social science to be interesting, and even helpful, in understanding the characteristic continuities of behavior. But his questions relate to another object, the divine Being. He might, however, wonder what patterns of Providence can be interpreted as present in the ordering of life that the student of social life describes. Or he might question whether both the continuing patterns and the particular actions of a person are in accord with what God has meant man to be in the world. The theologian's questions are governed by his concern—man in relation to God. The social scientist's questions are governed by his concern—man in relation to factors that condition or determine his behavior.

The response of some theologians to the social scientist's interpretation of man has been one of critical dismissal. The grounds for this seem to be the excessive confidence that many scientists have had, particularly in their assumptions

that what they have known provides grounds for predicta-
bility of behavior. Certainly most social scientists are now
cautious about predictions, though they would affirm that
their studies enable one to project certain probabilities with
reference to future behavior, both of persons and of groups.
Theologians also believe that the most important questions
about man cannot be answered by science, namely, those
that pertain to man's status before God and to man's moral
obligations to his neighbor. This is no doubt the case, but
within their limited sphere of concern, the scientists of behavior offer illuminating evidences.

Indeed, for the religious person, one of the functions of
genetic interpretations of man is to unmask illusions and
pretensions to which our faith tempts us. Christians are often
likely to assume that their behavior is governed by their
trust and loyalty to Jesus Christ, when the larger part of it
is actually determined by their relationships to parents and
to social groups. They are likely to assume that in faith they
are freed from bondage to their personal histories, to ideologies and groups, when in actual behavior they are not. Indeed,
the amount of light that social science can shed on behavior,
including the behavior of Christians, ought to chasten believers; it might lead them to self-examination and repentance. As Hannah Arendt, no friend of behaviorism as a
general philosophy, has observed, one reason the social scientists are so effective and popular in North America is that
so much of what they say about American behavior is true.
We do "behave" as conditioned, rather than "act" in the
light of reason or faith.

Man, the Creature of Needs and Desires

A basic model for the interpretation of human behavior
in a number of the social sciences has been taken from the

field of the biological sciences. It is the language of "organism," and if this word is rejected, part of its meaning is carried over into a "functional" theory. These terms point to a view of both individual selves and societies as entities that live for the sake of surviving with the least possible strain within and between persons and groups. Persons find ways of "adjusting" to what is happening to them, just as animals adapt to a changing physical environment. Societies seek to approximate a status of "equilibrium" in which the elements of conflict and dissent are reduced to a tolerable point, and something approaching harmony exists, just as in nature the various forces relate to each other in such a way that most beings and plants can survive. There are needs that have to be met, and human beings find ways to meet these needs. Indeed, for many sociologists, psychologists, and anthropologists man is finally an organism in an environment, seeking to establish those patterns of life that make for survival under the most harmonious conditions possible.

This view has been particularly offensive to many Christian interpreters of humanity, for it posits man and his survival as the final reality to which all things refer. Behavior has reference to God who created man, who requires man to meet certain conditions if life is to be sustained, who demands a faithfulness that might well bring the denial of harmony and equilibrium. Behavior is finally explainable with reference to need-fulfillment.

Functionalism readily becomes itself a pseudo-theological doctrine insofar as it provides a fundamental principle in the light of which almost everything is interpreted and understood. Religion itself, not to mention other phases of life and culture, is often explained on functional grounds. This has been done by a number of cultural anthropologists, and the viewpoint is by no means confined to the practitioners of that academic discipline or field. Bronislaw Malinowski was a major formulator of a functional theory. It is his view that man has a series of basic needs—for food, reproduction, bodily comfort, safety, growth, movement, and health. These needs in turn evoke developments in society and in culture. The need for food is at the root of agriculture, hunting, and fishing. These become the centers around which increasingly complicated institutions emerge: refinements in agricultural technology, development of marketing institutions, emergence of advertising, and many other things that a brief exercise of the imagination could enumerate. Even certain religious actions are related to this: in the uncertainty of the hunt or of crops, primitive tribes seek to relate themselves to the mysterious animistic powers that move all things, in order to remove obstacles that might hinder the enterprise. The need to reproduce evokes the intricacies of family systems, marriage, wider kinship groups, etc. These in turn find, among other things, religious sanctions; and ritual acts and beliefs like marriage services are brought to bear on sex and family life. Religion, like all other aspects of culture, is a human invention by which people manage to meet needs, and come to grips with the strains and tensions of life.[5]

Religion has also been interpreted in terms of society being "the substance of God." This view is associated with the name of Emile Durkheim,[6] and in a modified form has recently been developed in a book by sociologist Guy Swanson, *The Birth of the Gods*.[7] The God, or gods, function to provide a point of coherence, integration, and sanction for a society. A god is a projection of the "spirit" and the values of a society, and is given a reification in order to become an object of worship as well as a norm for behavior. Man, as religious being, then, fulfills a social need by the creation of religious rites and beliefs, which provide for the continuity of society as generations die and which become "collective representations" of the values and life of the community.

The notion of need-fulfillment also appears in treatises that deal with economic life and policy. In a very important study on *Politics, Economics, and Welfare*, Professors Robert Dahl and Charles Lindblom find it necessary to state the basic ends that are to be achieved in the policies of Western governments and societies. This obviously moves them into the realm of philosophical, ethical, and perhaps even theological questions. In accord with the general functionalism of the American human studies, however, they settle for "prime goals" that are basically need-fulfillment in their statement of them: "existence or survival, physiological gratifications (through food, sex, sleep, and comfort), love and affection, respect, self-respect, power or control, skill, enlightenment, prestige, aesthetic satisfaction, excitement, novelty and many others." [8] From these "prime goals" certain "instrumental goals" can be designated that define the particular ends to be sought through social policy, as well as the means to be considered in their achievement.

To what does economic behavior finally refer? To the needs of men. This, patently, is sensible. In the spheres of economics, politics, and much of social organization, all of which are in the realm of what theologians call "life in creation," the human needs have significance as a starting point, if not the point of final reference. No Christian interpreters of man would object to the value of preserving what is human, nor would they seek to divinize the natural in such a way that everything ought immediately to be related to the divine Presence and activity. Yet, this "functionalism" often tends to become the sole basis for the derivation of goals and norms for human behavior. If one wishes to find out what the proper goals for human life are, one looks to the things that people believe they need, to the things that they desire, to find them. If human beings desire variety in their sexual experience, then the order of sexual relations in which this is possible with the least stress and strain on their lives is the good order of human life.

Some critical moralists would acquiesce to the assertion that human needs form the fundamental basis of human morality, but would quarrel with particular determinations of what these needs are. A Roman Catholic might agree that what is right and good is what fulfills the deepest human needs, but he would hardly take a poll, or rely only on his observations of current behavior to determine what these needs are. He has a conviction that determines his definition of need, and in turn the ordering of life: namely, that man finally seeks the good and avoids evil; but the good is not simply the fulfillment of every desire, or the realization of impulses. To think about it properly one must introduce terms like justice, the virtues of prudence, temperance, and courage, and other things that are not derived from assessments based on analysis of behavioral evidence in some simple way.

The Roman Catholic, like other Christians, also would see the realm of human needs within a framework of God's creation, and of purposes that exist because God has so ordered human life. The point of stumbling is that most functional interpretations of man believe that there is no point of reference beyond the self or beyond nature, to which life refers. This becomes clear when a functional interpretation of religion comes into view. Religion has no point of reference that is objective to the needs of self and society. To speak of God is to speak of something that is incapable of empirical verification, whereas to speak of human needs is to define something which, men can agree, does exist. There is a "positivism" that informs functional views of man: only the observable, measurable man exists; he is not related to anything beyond himself. Man, in functionalism, is viewed only with reference to nature, and to nature defined in a particular way. Societies, like individual persons, seek an adjustment not to the will of God but to a state of equilibrium in which strains and tensions are reduced to the point of toleration.

The Christian might be most offended when he sees religion reduced to a human need, but he also ought to wonder whether economic and political life do not have some purpose with reference to the kind of life that God has created for men, to the kind of order through which God can sustain human societies. Where the functionalist stops is but a station in the Christian interpretation of man: God's work is done through the orders of preservation, the establishment of justice, the fulfillment of human potentialities.

Functionalism, however, cannot be lightly dismissed. Human needs are a kind of prism through which all light goes; for this reason functionalism can become an inclusive principle of explanation for human existence. Faith, Christians affirm, relates men to God, but faith in God also fulfills human longings and needs. Thus even faith goes through the prism of human need, man's need for God, and this provides the temptation to explain all that is involved in faith by that through which it is refracted. Further, when functionalism is applied to the interpretation of behavior, religious included, it has an unpleasant unmasking effect on the pretensions of Christians and other moral men. It enables men to see how much of action reputed to be engaged in for lofty purposes is really a matter of adjustment to the world. The functionalists provide a point of view for a critique of much religious life: We like to believe that men worship to praise God, but many of us worship to get a psychic serenity we need to adjust to the ambiguities of daily life. We like to believe that confirmation is a rite in which a child's reception into the Body of Christ by baptism is really confirmed, but for both parents and children it is often a puberty rite in which a new stage of physical and social maturity is celebrated. So much of behavior can be accounted for on functional grounds that it is no wonder the point of view has a persuasive power in contemporary culture.

Behavior Is Researchable

It is obvious that for many centuries scholars and poets, as well as businessmen and farmers, have been making observations of human behavior in which they have confidence, and from which they make certain generalizations. Aristotle made many shrewd remarks that seem to penetrate human behavior, such as "man is a political animal," and so have most philosophers. The fact that man can be "researched" is not novel. But some of the procedures used to research human behavior are increasingly refined in character. Among social scientists—sociologists, psychologists, political scientists, and others—the current effort is to find ways in which human behavior can be converted into numerical terms, can be recorded on IBM cards, and can be delineated in highly precise generalizations as a result of these refinements. One symptom of this is the way in which a course in statistics is required for most graduate students of society, persons, and politics. It is as if the way to reality was by the quantification of things, and unfortunately in some instances the assumption is that if something is not reducible to number it is not researchable, and therefore (almost) it is not real.

These refined measurements of behavior are not without significant value, although they are probably overvalued by some of the researchers. Certainly they are a rigorous check upon impressions; persons who assume that they can perceive and generalize on human behavior have often merely projected what they wish to see onto the world around them. No longer need this be the case; the perceptions and imaginative generalizations can become the hypotheses for more careful assessment of what is and is not the case. For example, for generations there have been assumptions about the political behavior of various social groups in the United States, based on impressions from election returns. If a particular ward was heavily Democratic, and there was a large Roman Catholic Church in the ward, men felt rather secure in saying that Roman Catholics vote Democratic. And they were probably correct. But with various sampling techniques, refined schedules of inquiry, etc., one can find out not only how many Roman Catholics vote Democratic, but whether other factors are not more important than the religious one, e.g., the income status, the ethnic group identification, the family system, and the like. General impressions are corrected and refined by research into political behavior.

The measurement research into behavior professes to be interested only in accurate description of what exists. Description includes not only an account of what is at any particular time and place, but also an analysis of the correlation of factors that enable one to begin to understand some reasons why "what is" is. Thus, there is an easy movement from description to causal analysis, and at this point other questions sometimes need to be raised. First, if the methods of measurement begin to dictate what can be researched, can one be sure he is finding out the most important things that need to be known about behavior? This question might be answered by various social scientists in different ways. The more modest and self-critical might suggest that all one gets at are certain indices of behavior, and that these are limited to some extent by the number of variables the researcher seeks to ferret out in his research design. Even when one can make significant correlations between aspects of human life, one has not yet proved a causal sequence. Less self-critical practitioners of the measurement procedures often claim more for what they find out; crudely stated, they assume that if something is not quantifiable it is not real, and in effect rather than conforming method to the human behavior to be studied, they rule out the significance of all behavior that cannot be reduced to their methods. At its worst, this kind of work is mechanical, presumptuous, and "genius-proof."

Second, there is a great deal of dubiety in assuming that correlations declare unambiguously clear assertions of causation. Robert Merton, in refining the procedures for the sociology of knowledge, suggests some of the words that need to be carefully selected in determining the character of the relationship of things that are correlated: they "correspond" to each other; or one is the "condition" of the other, or there is a "functional interdependence" between them, or one "determines" the other.[9] In the selection of appropriate words, there is a heavy weight of philosophical decision, of predisposition, that is not necessarily verifiable, or requires even more refined studies to validate accurately. For example, juvenile delinquents in one area are Negroes, Protestants, come from lower-income families, have a high incidence of broken families, live in slums, and are poorly educated. In another area they are white, Roman Catholic, of Italian extraction, from families with lower incomes, have traditional Italian family systems, etc. How does one assess which factors are "causally" most significant in delinquency? There are refined ways to proceed with such analysis and, without doubt, through social analysis one can be surer about which factors are more important than one can be without social analysis. But judgments have to be made, even of the data, and these obviously require more than measurement—a fact social scientists would agree to. But social analysis of behavior is not prejudice-proof; one can be disposed to look at Protestant religious behavior, for example, as the result of large segments being members of the middle class; but a case is also made for the fact that Protestant religious faith and life tends to push people toward middle-class goals and behavior. I merely wish to indicate the complexity that is involved in making judgments of causality between factors of behavior that are significantly correlated statistically.

The Christian interpreter can be informed about what is actually taking place by the work of social research. He often wonders if what he finds out is worth all the time, effort, and money that went into such study, but that query is not so much the result of his Christian viewpoint as it is of other bases of judgment. But the Christian interpreter generally wonders whether the most significant dimensions of human behavior can be reduced to the measurement procedures. Some things that formerly seemed out of the range of research now are coming into it, for example, research on the "values" that people hold, and the extent to which behavior is governed by them. But can something like loving the neighbor be measured? If one could get consensus on which acts are "loving" acts, which attitudes are "loving" attitudes, etc., something might be done. But insofar as love of neighbor is a spontaneous act, stemming from God's gracious love, and freely given to the other, perhaps the task is more difficult if not impossible.

Further, Christians have believed that man is related to God (a "nonempirical factor" for social research). There are dimensions of the meaning of human behavior that are governed by faith in God. It is at this level of the framework for interpreting the *meaning* of human existence that Christians part company with the social researcher. This parting of the ways does not mean a rejection of what research has found out, but a critical approach to it, seeking to make clear the assumptions of such research. It also requires that the Christian interpreters carefully develop the significance of what is known about man through research, for the moral and theological purposes that are given in the Christian community. The data are interpreted with reference to the knowledge of God and his will and work.

Similarly, the secular ethicist might be grateful for information on voting behavior, but he necessarily incorporates other bases for judgment and interpretation into his efforts to define what political and social policies are "good" for a given society. The research may help him at the level of tactics for achievement of moral ends, if he wills to put policy into action, but he has other purposes in view and thus reinterprets what is known. Max Millikan, in an essay "Inquiry and Policy," suggests that what the researcher comes out with in his conclusions is not so important for the policymaker as are his arguments. "The purpose of social science research should be to deepen, broaden, and extend the policymaker's capacity for judgment—not to provide him with answers." [10] Obviously, then, the measurement research into behavior is worthwhile if the problems to which it is addressed are important, and if it needs to be used by Christian and secular interpreters of man. But the moral judgments that go into policy judgments cannot be derived from research.

What is the Christian's response to the general views of man in the social sciences? Properly, first it is gratitude for the kinds of knowledge and understanding of human behavior that can be derived from the perspectives and procedures that inform the social scientist. He sees things because he has a particular view; he depicts behavior because he has refined procedures to use. But the Christian's response is also critical—though certainly not rejection. He is critical of claims made indiscreetly that all there is to know of man can be known from the scientific perspective and method. But such a critique must be discriminatingly applied only to those social scientists who assume the posture of omniscience. The Christian claims the right to interpret man from the Christian perspective as well, and he sees things in this light that the lights from social science do not expose. Finally, the Christian carefully interprets and uses the knowledge from the social sciences in his own particular interpretations of men, and in his ethical considerations. For the Christian is interested in the quality of human life and in the moral character of human action.

4

A Christian Critique
of Secular Anthropologies

by Keith R. Bridston

Any "Christian critique" of modern secular anthropologies must be entered into with the greatest trepidation, indeed humility. Herbert Butterfield in *Christianity and History* has pointed out that Christians have all too often stood on the wrong side of controversies in which ecclesiastical authorities felt the "Christian" cause was at stake: "Sometimes, indeed, as in the case of freedom of conscience, the Church has bitterly fought the world, and I am confronted by the anomaly that it was the world which stood for the cause now regarded as the right one even by the clergy themselves." [1]

This is a peculiarly subtle temptation when questions having to do with the nature of man and his destiny are under consideration. Christians, I suppose, have every right to make statements, even dogmatic affirmations, about man. But the proper biblical preface to these is a searching question: "What is man?" And the ultimate answer to that question lies not in our affirmations, but in God's answer. That, of course, lies in the mystery of God himself, in his love and grace. Thus, to a certain extent, man—even Christian man —cannot finally and definitively answer the Psalmist's question: "What is man?" Only God really knows.

To compare Christian anthropology with secular anthropology or anthropologies, therefore, is not to compare the absolute with relatives. If there is indeed a "true" Christian anthropology, there is no guarantee that Christians are the ones articulating it at the moment. Our problem is to find who is, and then to appropriate it.

The first clue, and perhaps the decisive one, is the concern for man as man. Presumably in the Christian tradition this might be taken for granted. Ironically it cannot be. Particularly since the time of the Reformation, and especially within the Western Christian tradition, the doctrine of sin has been so understood and interpreted as to cast doubt on the worth and meaning of man as man. The extreme form of this doctrinal bias is contained in the idea of "total depravity," but the fundamental pessimism of this anthropological perspective is largely shared in Western Christianity and may have infected the whole of the Church's view of man in all parts of Christendom today.

This radical pessimism in regarding man is, of course, a "protestant" corrective, but like all correctives it tends itself to become absolutized. To say that man is sinful is to say the obvious. Sometimes, to be sure, the obvious needs to be stated. This has often been true in the history of Christianity: a great many reform movements, not to speak of revolutions, are so explainable. Unfortunately, the idea crept in that to assert the sinfulness of man was necessary to uphold the authority, power, and majestic holiness of God. Christian theologians began to be protective about God, and they paternalistically defended him by deprecating man. What could be more futile, or what could demonstrate more effectively the subtlety of sin itself in inflating human pretensions! But above all, this compulsive concern to protect God by denying man resulted in a denial of two of the most basic foundation stones of the Christian tradition: first, that God created man, and in his own image; second, that God so loved man, even as sinful and fallen, that he gave himself to restore man to his true and proper state.

In short, Christian anthropology has been in its present forms largely informed by the doctrine of sin, at the expense of the doctrine of creation, and determined by an obsession with justification without adequate grounding in the Incarnation. Hendrik Kraemer, the great missiologist, has described Islam as "super-heated" monotheism,* but the same inclination toward an exaggerated theocentricity may be found in Christian thought as well. The New Testament itself bears ample witness to the fact that to love God who is not seen is easier for most than to love man who is seen. That is particularly true when it is thought that to love God somehow makes the love of neighbor only relatively important.

Against this background, it may perhaps be more understandable why so-called "secular" anthropologies have to be taken with the utmost seriousness by any Christian who wishes to know what "true" anthropology is. Insofar as they are concerned with man as man they may already have exceeded the rightness of much that passes for "Christian anthropology" in many of the theologies of the Church, both past and present.

Furthermore, besides being correctives to defective and inadequate "Christian" anthropologies, secular views of man may in themselves incarnate and articulate essential elements necessary for the recovery of the full image of man revealed

---

* "Islam is theocentric, but in a super-heated state. Allah in Islam becomes white-hot Majesty, white-hot Omnipotence, white-hot Uniqueness. His personality vanishes in the burning heat of His aspects. . . . Man is entirely absorbed in the greatness and majesty of God and vanishes away" (*Christian Message in a Non-Christian World* [Grand Rapids, Mich.: Kregel, 1961], pp. 221-222).

in the Bible, but elements which have been lost or forgotten in the Christian tradition down through the centuries. This does not mean that the spokesmen for such positions are always conscious of the anthropological implications of their insights. Indeed, one of the weaknesses of many secular anthropologies is their fragmentary and "sectarian" character. They discover a truth, or a valid interpretation, but often emphasize it to the exclusion of all others. The "truth" about man must be catholic; that is, it must incorporate all valid insights into one anthropology. Unless the Christian doctrine of man has this catholic character it cannot be "true" in the full and complete sense of that word, however well it is attested by tradition or bolstered by dogmatic authority.

It would take much more space than is available here merely to describe, to say nothing of criticizing, the various secular anthropologies that are current today. In examining these contemporary views of man, nevertheless, it is apparent that the most vital and important of them have their origins in some of the great pivotal thinkers of the nineteenth century: Darwin, Marx, and Freud. It is perhaps worth noting that, considered in the perspectives of universal history, these great "originals" who are the architects of our modern thought-world are intimately related to the Christian tradition, however alienated they may have been from the religious establishments of their day. In fact, the growth of the "new mentality" of science which all three so brilliantly represent and which, as Whitehead puts it, "has practically recoloured our mentality," in a very real sense finds its source, to use John Baillie's words, in "the Christian doctrine of creation" and "the Christian doctrine that the order of nature is contingent upon the divine Will." [2]

Deny it as they will, secular thinkers are indelibly marked

with the Christian stamp and this is most transparent in their anthropological views. It is another reason, of course, why what they have to say is so important in reconstructing a modern Christian doctrine of man. These great "outsiders" represent the primitive Christian memory like a multifaceted mirror held up before the Christian community of today. The reflections of the various mirrors, distorted and obscure in different ways, together help to indicate the true Christian anthropological image.

It may be that the chief criticism which can be leveled against the secular anthropologies of our day is not that they fail to take "Christian" anthropology seriously, or even that they are "unreligious," but that they are subconsciously inhibited from working out the full logic of their discoveries because they *think* (or, better, unconsciously *feel*) that their insights are "unchristian" or "unreligious"; for in the marrow of their spiritual bones they are religious and Christian. The theological framework which they have accepted as orthodox, and which has been confirmed by the attacks of Christian critics, has no place for the truths which they have found. And, as a result, both they and the Christian intellectual community have been poorer for it; they have been intellectually excommunicated and they have accepted that excommunication as valid. If the advocates of secular anthropologies have tended to be sectarian, it is partly because Christian defenders have refused to let them be catholic.

This may be illustrated by returning to the great germinal thinkers already mentioned. Each of those named (and there are others almost equally worthy of mention were space to permit) has many aspects to his thought. All that can be done here is to suggest the chief contribution which each has made to current anthropological views.

Man as Natural

Darwin has made the point that man is natural. The Copernican and Cartesian revolutions had destroyed the "bandbox affair" of the neatly ordered medieval world, including its angelic hosts and prankish devils, and the result was that "man was alone, quite alone, in a vast and complex cosmic machine." [3] But there was still place for a faith that man was special, that he was somehow not a part of the machine, and that God had made it all for him. Darwin, however, along with Spencer, Thomas Huxley, and the other evolutionists shattered even that thin remnant of faith in man's natural uniqueness. Man was simply the highest and most complicated form of life resulting from an evolutionary process starting from the simplest protozoon. As Darwin himself put it:

Not only the various domestic races, but the most distinct genera and orders within the same great class—for instance, mammals, birds, reptiles, and fishes—are all the descendants of one common progenitor, and we must admit that the whole vast amount of difference between these forms has primarily arisen from simple variability. To consider the subject under this point of view is enough to strike one dumb with amazement.[4]

Darwin did not devote much time to the metaphysical implications of his theory, but there were many who did. And it was not so much the facts of evolution as the theory of it which, in various forms and applied to many fields, has made an enormous impact on intellectual history since that time. As has been mentioned, the apparent reduction of man to one integral element in the general evolution of life struck defenders of the Christian faith with amazement, but not dumbness. In Roman Catholicism, for example, only recently through Teilhard de Chardin has this basic hostility and defensiveness given way to an attempt to appropriate evolutionary theory as a fundamental structure for theological speculation.

But if Darwinism seemed to reduce man's spiritual stature and uniqueness, modern physics carried this undermining of traditional Christian anthropology even further—so far, in fact, that the circle may have been completed. Evolutionary theory, after all, could be viewed as a vivid testimony to the intellectual powers of man, whatever his biological origins. Modern physics, however, has thrown doubts on even that. It is not only that man appears much smaller and more insignificant when looked at in a cosmic perspective. Even more significant, physicists' cosmological speculations deriving from Einstein have ended in a radical skepticism about the ability of man to comprehend the natural universe; P. W. Bridgman says of this development:

Finally, I come to what seems to me may well be from the long range point of view the most revolutionary of the insights to be derived from our recent experiences in physics, more revolutionary than the insights afforded by the discoveries of Galileo and Newton, or of Darwin. This is the insight that it is impossible to transcend the human reference point. . . . The new insight comes from the realization that the structure of nature may eventually be such that our processes of thought do not correspond to it sufficiently to permit us to think about it all. We have already had an intimation of this in the behavior of very small things in the quantum domain. . . . There can be no difference of opinion with regard to the dilemma that now confronts us in the direction of the very small. We are now approaching a bound beyond which we are forever stopped from pushing our inquiries, not by the construction of the world, but by the construction of ourselves. The world fades out and eludes us because it becomes meaningless. We cannot even express this in the way we would like. We cannot say that there exists a world beyond any knowledge possible to us because of the nature of knowledge. The very concept of existence becomes meaningless. It is literally true that the only way of reacting to this is to shut up. We are confronted with something truly ineffable. We have reached the limit of vision of the great pioneers of science, namely that we live in a sympathetic world, in that it is comprehensible by our minds.[5]

Is this saying somewhat the same thing that Christian theologians mean when they speak of the mystery of God's creation? Groups of physicists and theologians in Germany have begun a dialogue on precisely this question. Though it is premature to suggest that at long last the thought-worlds of science and theology have begun to meet, one physicist-theologian seems to believe a confluence is immanent, particularly in regard to their respective views of man. As C. F. von Weizsäcker suggests in *The History of Nature* the skepticism and nihilism reflected in the words of Bridgman are in some sense "the negative counterpole of Christianity" and "when this experience faces its own situation fully, it is perhaps the most honest self-appraisal of the modern world." [6] Or to put it another way, a full recognition of man's identity with the natural universe has eventually led not to a pretentious magnification of man, but to a recognition that man in a microcosmic way is "truly ineffable." He is to himself a mystery. It may be cause for reflection that the empirical scientists are saying this with more conviction than some theologians for whom the question "What is man?" apparently has been exhaustively answered by their theomonistic dogmatic categories.

Man as Social

Marx has made the point that man is social. Herbert Spencer's application of Darwinism to society and history suggests the easy compatibility between Darwin's empirical evolutionary data and the general climate of optimistic progressivism of the nineteenth century. Marx was both a product and a creator of that philosophical spirit of inevitable human advance. Darwin, Marx, and Freud were all concerned with the dynamics of life and, though their theories were not directly connected with one another, they had this in common: "Each emphasized the extent to which the human being is the product of forces outside his control." [7] In this sense they were all—implicitly or explicitly—protesting against the Hegelian idealism dominating the preceding era which tended to explain all human dynamics as derivative from reason.

Marxism accepts Hegelian rationalism to the extent of borrowing its dialectical method but, as Marx himself proclaimed, he had taken the thesis-antithesis-synthesis pyramid which Hegel had foolishly tried to balance on its idealistic point and placed it squarely on its base: materialistic historical determinism. Darwin indicated that man was formed by his biological origins, and Marx supplemented this environmental determinism by focusing on the economic factor, "the means of production," as decisive in the formation of man. Marxist theory is largely occupied with the riddle of social change—a riddle which the economic and technological revolution of the nineteenth century imposed on every perceptive thinker of the time, however different their answers to it. My old friend David Carmichael's *bon mot,* "Read Marx and inwardly digest," is particularly appropriate for Christians because, of all the answers given to the nineteenth century's riddle of change, the Church's tended to be the most romantic and individualistic. Though there were some notable exceptions (such as F. D. Maurice), through its hymns, tracts, sermons, and theological books the nineteenth-century Christian community taken as a whole reflects two extremes: utopian idealism and spiritualized pietism. In both cases, it is man as an individual who is the center of attention and upon whom the theological fulcrum rests. It may be the world which is to be saved, or man himself, but in either case it depends upon the efforts of individuals. Man understood in a corporate sense is almost entirely missing.

The idea of individuality "which is the most unique emphasis of modern culture," according to Reinhold Niebuhr, and has deep Christian roots, is a "tragically abortive concept" when it becomes ideologically rationalized into secular individualism.[8] But this is precisely the distinguishing mark of nineteenth-century Christian anthropology. And though it may have passed in theological circles, this individualistic understanding of man still remains potent in the Christian community in a vestigial way through "popular" religion in local congregations. The fact that man cannot be understood apart from his fellows, that his corporate environment determines his individual significance, that his social setting and relationships define his manhood—points which St. Paul makes with some force to the Church in Corinth—has yet fully to penetrate the mentality of the Christian community even though the secular community has mainly accepted and absorbed it. Needless to say, Marx's social anthropology may be all too congenial to the collectivist tendencies of modern life whether that is seen in political dictatorship or communal conformism. But any Christian critique to be made of these centripetal forces on the basis of man's dignity and integrity as an individual can only be undertaken if the essential social and corporate character of the Christian message is affirmed at the same time.

The increased attention being given by theologians to

ecclesiology in recent years may indicate a change toward a more social orientation in Christian anthropology as well. Nevertheless, the forming and deforming impact of corporate "principalities and powers" on man's being has been given much more perceptive analyses by social critics such as William Whyte in *The Organization Man*, C. Northcote Parkinson in his tongue-in-cheek *Parkinson's Law*, Vance Packard, C. Wright Mills, and other "popular" sociologists in their various writings than by the theological moralists representing the religious Establishment. Only recently have Christian spokesmen such as Gibson Winter and James M. Gustafson and Liston Pope shown evidence of having absorbed the anthropological insight of man as social thoroughly enough to *think* Christian ethics naturally in sociological terms. But this natural sociological-theological integration has not yet affected the general anthropological ethos of the churches. Social problems are increasingly being recognized as social, but the criteria used to judge them and the antidotes being suggested are largely individualistic. And so the pressing moral issues being imposed by a collectivist age—from invasion of privacy to automation—are being denied relevant Christian analysis. This discrepancy between the social form in which modern man is meeting his most excruciating moral crises and the individualistic anthropological bias of local "folk" Christianity may be one of the chief explanations why ministers are facing traumatic frustrations in effectively communicating through their preaching today.

Man as Visceral

Freud has made the point that man is visceral. In considering the revolutionary implications of his work, Freud compared himself to both Copernicus and Darwin; and in his writings he not infrequently mentioned Marx and referred to his concepts. Whether Freud, as an intellectual revolutionary, will eventually be ranked as a true Copernican is probably premature to say; nevertheless, his own estimate of the tremendous impact of his theories on the imagination of twentieth-century man is difficult to dismiss. In fact, there are those who argue: "Two figures stand out massively as the architects of our present-day conception of man: Darwin and Freud." [9] And as with Darwin, the empirical biologist, so with Freud, the practicing neurologist, his influence may be ascribed as much—perhaps even more—to the conclusions drawn from, and the philosophical meaning attached to, his laboriously achieved research data than the scientific theories he himself developed from it.

Freud's work is too rich and multidimensioned to be quickly and briefly summarized. In thinking of its impact on our modern secular view of man, however, one thing stands out: Freud made crystal clear the incalculable significance of the largely submerged portion of human nature for a proper understanding of man. Whatever names one wishes to attach to that hidden realm—passion, emotion, instinct, unconscious force—Freud branded upon the popular mind the fact that this mysterious, hidden world was "reality," that it actually existed, and that it was mightily determinative of who men were and what they were and how they were as human beings.

The word "sex" is commonly associated with Freud. Symbolically, at least, that word may be as apt as any in epitomizing Freud's anthropological contribution, however oversimplified it may be to describe his whole thought. For it was through his isolation of sexuality as an "energy of equal dignity," as the power behind a neurosis, that "Freud would soon be able to describe psychic reality systematically as the domain of phantasy, dream, and mythology, and as the imagery and language of a universal unconscious, and thus adding as a scientific dimension to the image of man what had been an age-old intuitive knowledge." [10] In short, Freud broke through the inhibitions, prudery, and hypocrisy of the Victorian mentality camouflaging the true nature of man and subjected it to naked scientific examination and inquiry.

If Freud's theory of sex tended to overshoot its mark, or to be too simplistic, nevertheless it was, in the religious reaction it provoked, a vivid reminder of the fact that "it was only too easy to do what had become civilization's 'second nature,' that is, in the face of man's sexual and aggressive drives ever again to beat a hasty retreat into romanticism and religionism, into secrecy, ridicule, and lechery," as Erik Erikson says. That is, Freud's insights into human nature are a perennial warning against anthropological falsifications in the name of supposed religious or theological principles or scruples.

It is all too easy to understand why the Church found Freudian anthropology difficult to digest, and may still find it so. For one thing, Christian theology since the time of the Reformation has tended to be docetic. That can be seen in Christology as well as ecclesiology. The incarnational affirmation that the "Word became flesh" does not come easily to those who presuppose a basic and unalterable dichotomy between spirit and matter. When this dualistic mentality applies itself to a description of man, the outcome is foreordained: *essential* man is a spirit or—as in idealism—a mind. At the same time, the churches on the whole are Marcionite—in practice if not in theory. The "earthiness" of the Old Testament has little attraction for spiritualized Christians, and the liturgical (as well as the educational and homiletical) practice of the churches bears witness to this fact. Phrases such as "I long after you all in the bowels of

Christ" fall on deaf ears; and if not deaf, faintly scandalized. "Bowels," after all, are hardly proper and certainly not to be thought of as the abode of religious "spiritual" feelings. "Well, the early Christians were somewhat crude and primitive in other ways as well." So we are inclined to leave speculation about bowels and their relation to the nature of man to the psychologists and cultural anthropologists in their theories of infantile sexuality and toilet training.

This Marcionite-docetic truncation of Christian anthropology has had disastrous consequences. Christian theology itself, cut off from the emotional warmth, the vivid imagery, and the essential humanity of the Jewish tradition as found in the Old Testament, becomes dry, dogmatic, and unimaginative; it is an exercise of the head, a cerebral enterprise which in its scholastic rigidity cannot comprehend a Joseph whose "bowels did yearn upon his brother" or whose rough intellectual instruments cannot discern the intricate human interplay between Saul, David, and Jonathan. Such spiritualized and rationalized "Christian" anthropology is incapable of coping with man as man; it can only do so when man has been reduced to its cramped theological measure.

Is it surprising, then, that "no one can count the number of people who now think of any crisis as a personal failure, and who turn to a psychoanalyst or to a psychoanalytical literature for an explanation of their suffering where once they would have turned to a minister or to the Bible for consolation"? [11] Beyond these more immediate pastoral implications, the shriveled anthropology falsely called "Christian" has led our whole culture to seek elsewhere than in the Church for the meaning of life and of man. Modern man does not go to hear a sermon if he is perplexed about his nature and being: he goes to see Bergman's or Fellini's films, he sees Albee's or Osborne's plays, he reads Camus, Faulkner, Joyce, or Sartre. This is not to say that he is going to find in Fellini's "8½" or in Williams' *Night of the Iguana* the final answer to his perplexities; but at least he knows that his question "What is man?" is also theirs and that they are willing to be open to all the paradoxical dimensions of human existence in searching out a viable answer. The same cannot be said for many sermons.

In much the same way, in the field of science and in the political sphere, so-called "Christian" anthropology has by its diminutive character forced out both honest speculation and rigorous action from the religious community. In view of this melancholy history, the Christian critique of secular anthropologies must, as was mentioned at the beginning of this essay, be preceded by radical repentance. That in turn must be followed by the recognition that the very idea of a "Christian" anthropology set over against "secular" views is a false understanding of the problem. The Christian view of man, if it is true, cannot be one among many. Its truth lies precisely in its catholicity: that is, in its ability to comprehend all valid anthropological truths and see them as a whole. The fact that the elemental anthropological insights "man is natural," "man is social," "man is visceral" have had such tardy recognition by Christians (especially when these particular insights are so intimately related to the mainstream of the Judaeo-Christian theological tradition) should be an evident warning against complacency about the ease with which this synthesizing and integrating task may be accomplished.

Ernst Cassirer in *An Essay on Man* expresses dismay that the variety of empirical treatments of man resulted in a situation in which "our modern theory of man lost its intellectual center. We acquired instead a complete anarchy of thought." In the past, he writes, metaphysics, theology, mathematics, and biology successively gave guidance in integrating anthropological thought, but the "real crisis of this problem manifested itself when such a central power capable of directing all individual efforts ceased to exist; . . . an established authority to which one might appeal no longer existed. Theologians, scientists, politicians, sociologists, biologists, psychologists, ethnologists, economists all approached the problem from their own viewpoint. To combine or unify all these particular aspects and perspectives was impossible." [12] Cassirer finds it ironical that precisely at the time when we have a superabundance of facts derived from scientific investigation, when our instruments for observation and experimentation have become sharper, and in general when we have a more favorable position than any other age for a penetrating view of man, we appear "nevertheless, not yet to have found a method for the mastery and organization of this material."

Cassirer quotes Max Scheler to the same effect: "In no other period of human knowledge has man ever become more problematic to himself than in our own days. We have a scientific, a philosophical, and a theological anthropology that know nothing of each other. Therefore we no longer possess any clear and consistent idea of man. The ever-growing multiplicity of the particular sciences that are engaged in the study of men has much more confused and obscured than elucidated our concept of man." [13]

What are Christians to say, then, when confronted by a Julian Huxley who says that "man represents the culmination of that process of organic evolution which has been proceeding on this planet for over a thousand million years" and that his unique value ultimately lies in the fact that "man has now become the sole representative of life in that progressive aspect and its sole trustee for any progress in the future"?[14] Or when Marx speaks through one of his disciples, saying, "Man is an ensemble of social relations"? Or when a D. H. Lawrence proclaims, "My great religion is a belief in the blood, the flesh, as being wiser than the intellect. We can go wrong in our minds. But what our blood feels and believes, and says, is always true"? What is the Christian response?

As has been suggested, the first inclination is simply to disprove such anthropological positions, critically to undermine and dismember them, and then to substitute the "true" doctrine in their place. Or it is to try to synthesize them within a grander and more comprehensive conceptual framework. It may be, however, that this assumption of intellectual superiority is not only outmoded but actually futile for Christian theologians. Cassirer and Scheler may be quite right in placing theology as one among many competing anthropological viewpoints, none of which can hope to provide the intellectual integrating center for the rest. Theology as a scientific discipline cannot expect to be given a special intellectual edge in open scientific competition.

But is the Christian image of man ultimately a conceptual framework, an intellectual idea, a doctrine? Is there, in fact, a Christian anthropology at all? The Christian view of man is derived from an image, not an idea. It is drawn from and projected by a person, not a dogma. When Christians confess "true man," they do not define him, they behold him. They do not intellectualize about him, they believe in him.

This, of course, is not anthropology but faith. It is probably absurd to think that faith can be a critique of all other anthropologies. But is it more absurd than to think that man ultimately can be his own measure? Or to believe that any anthropology, even a theological anthropology, can ever take the full measure of this True Man?

He came to fulfill, not to destroy, the law and the prophets. He still comes to do the same. That is his final human critique. And it must be ours.

5

The Secular Challenge to the Christian View

by D. G. Brown

The secular challenge to what exactly? To the traditional
Christian conception of man. But does Christian belief have
a conception of man which is either peculiar to it or inseparable from it? Nathan Scott says, in the first essay of this book,
that man is created in the image of God, is fallen, and is
restored by Christ for life within the community of the
Church in the service of others. This picture, when refracted
through my secular mind, splits into two parts. One part
contains psychological and moral insights which have great
value, though not unique value, and which are capable of
making their own way along with those of Plato, or with
those of Hobbes and Winstanley, Rousseau and Hume, Freud
and Marx. A conception of man is certainly projected. His
divided nature, his limitations and his vulnerability, his
capacities for love, rationality and evil, his social role—all
these are sketched. If I turn as well to scriptural or Thomistic
or liberal Protestant versions of Christian belief, these project
a variety of conceptions of man. But even where the pictures
are drawn from Jesus himself they remain psychological and
moral, they are accessible to anyone, and they can and must
commend themselves on their own merits to secular experience and secular insight.

89

What then is the other part of the picture? What is left, which the secular mind deflects to a separate screen for separate contemplation? It is that special light in which origin becomes creation, creative historical action becomes supernatural intervention, and our ideals become Another's purposes. Here I find not what we are like, but how we came to exist. Not demands and ideals, but Whose purposes these reflect. Not an exploration of our own resources, but a reassurance about the intelligibility of the universe. Not our character, but a drama in which we are characters. All this is recognizably Christian, but there is a sense in which it is not about us. It is the background in the picture of man, not the figure of man himself. Theology is not anthropology.

So there is, it may appear, a conception of man which the secular person is glad to come to terms with, but which is not irreducibly Christian. There is also, segregated and ripe for rejection, a set of characteristic theological doctrines which do not concern man himself, and whose falsity or emptiness would not concern any man whose concern was man. Surely the cunning of the secular mind must lie precisely in those admirable prisms and lenses, by which it appropriates for its own image of man anything in the Christian tradition which pleases it, and filters out anything transcendent and supernatural—filters out God.

It may seem to the believer that the rejection of Christian faith, or the profession of inability to grasp its content, comes easily enough as a sequel to such preparation. For the preparation seems to consist in presuming the self-sufficiency of a secular view of man, and in presenting as an undistorted image of him a picture from which his relation to God is left out. It is not that the unbeliever rejects a view of man which the Christian offers him. His perennial strategy is to take it over, insofar as it is strictly a view of man, and then to ask what belief in God could add to it. The question is whether he can legitimately do this. Are there not definite consequences for one's view of man which flow from faith in God and are not available from any other source? How can the secular point of view accept each Christian insight, and yet incur no theological debt?

Here we encounter the first of two main issues I will examine in this essay. I want to argue that the secular person can accomplish this appropriation while remaining on his own ground, and that this is precisely the strength of his position. It would be understandable if the believer found no matter for irritation so deeply frustrating as the combination, in secular minds, of a hospitable exploitation of Christian insights, Christian art, and Christian social action, wherever these made their way in the secular world, together with a genuine, calm, complete lack of interest in anything theological. It would be forgivable if the believer were to diagnose this attitude as complacency, and accuse this complacency of extending to the historical and political predicaments men are now in. But I will argue that the believer would be in error. The secular point of view really has become all-embracing. It now claims all the great words: inspiration, revelation; salvation, damnation; the godlike and the devilish; it has domesticated them all. It has relegated God to its etymologies without losing an intelligible concept.

That this is so is of course a controversial thesis. In the next section of this chapter I will undertake to explain and recommend it. Evidently there is just one line of argument open to me. The only way in which the secular point of view can become all-embracing is for the nonsecular point of view to diminish to vanishing point. My thesis will be that the apparently overweening claims of the nonbeliever are a reflection of the vacuousness of the believer's claims.

It follows that there is no head-on clash between Christian belief and a secular conception of man. On the one hand, the nontheological part of the beliefs of those who happen to be Christians includes beliefs about human nature which are commonly shared by nonbelievers. Where they conflict with characteristically anti-Christian views, the conflict is no more essential or predictable than the many conflicts within the secular world, between Marxists and existentialists or between Freudians and behaviorists. In any case, contemporary Christian doctrine tends increasingly to adopt modern insights into human nature.

On the other hand, the theological part of Christian belief receives no direct comment from the empirical study of human nature. The secular attack on belief in God is philosophical, not scientific. It seems in fact to be generally agreed that psychological, sociological, and historical accounts of the origins and conditions of religious belief do not constitute evidence for or against its rational acceptability. In sum, the secular view of man comes into direct and essential conflict neither with the theological nor with the nontheological aspects of Christian belief.

But if this is so, how is it that we all recognize, in the Darwinian, Marxian, Freudian, and Sartrean views of human nature and society, currents of thought which are powerfully corrosive of Christian belief? If the empirical study of religious belief as a human phenomenon is in principle irrelevant to its rational claims, it becomes mysterious why the formation of the superego and the origins of sacrificial cults seem more damaging to theology than does the invalidity of the argument from design. Here we encounter the second of the two main issues I propose to examine. This ambivalence about the relation between rational criticism and empirical explanation is widespread in contemporary discussions. More than one rationalist prides himself on recognizing that psychological origins are irrelevant, and on continuing a fair-minded examination of the rational claims of theological doctrine, only to be overtaken by the guilty awareness that the empirical facts impress him enormously; he then feels subject to an illicit, merely ideological kind of persuasion. More than one Christian believer stands pat on the independence of the theological issues, or grants to psychology the power to purify belief by unmasking its spurious forms, only to feel unnerved nevertheless by secular accounts of human nature. I want to argue that the rational criticism of beliefs is indeed logically prior to the empirical explanation of them, and that questions of causal explanation only arise when rational justification breaks down and a belief has thereby been shown to be irrational. But I will also try to show that in an intellectually satisfying account of the phenomena of belief, the machinery of rational reconstruction and of causal explanation must mesh together exactly. The empirical sciences must take over just where rational criticism calls them in. When this meshing occurs, the conviction carried by both accounts is sharply intensified. I will argue that the persuasive force of the secular accounts of human nature, in unsettling theological belief, is due to the philosophical preparation of their point of contact. Once again, it is the gradual and subtle emptying of theological doctrine under philosophical criticism which has opened the explanatory role to empirical studies of belief. When doctrines become vacuous rather than false, their loss of claim upon rational assent is less conspicuous. But the occasion for causal explanation, and the conviction carried by such explanation, are just as great. A philosophical demonstration of its vacuousness, and an empirical explanation of its occurrence, are together unanswerably destructive of the appeal of any belief.

For this reason, the over-all effect of this essay may well be felt as a secular attack on the traditional Christian conception of man. But I have tried to explain how obliquely I must approach the enterprise. My critique consists in examining the two issues I have identified, and in propounding a thesis about each. My first thesis is that the residue of Christian belief left by philosophical criticism has become vacuous, and that by its correlative expansion the secular point of view has become all-embracing. Its critique of Christian views of man therefore consists merely in filtering out the theological component and dealing with the rest within the ordinary secular debate. My second thesis is that modern secular insights into the nature of man, though they have a powerful influence in the undermining of theological belief, achieve this influence indirectly. Empirical understanding of the conditions of religious belief, though not in principle relevant to rational criticism, supplements and reinforces the philosophical critique. Curiously perhaps, this philosopher finds the source of both theses in that conceptual analysis of theological doctrines by which their lack of content is exhibited.

Is There a Christian Conception of Man?

In examining the extent to which the secular view has become all-embracing we should first attend to a point that is easy to acknowledge formally, less easy to accept emotionally. Historical debt is not logical debt. The identification of ideas as Christian in origin is a historical matter which does not prejudge the dependence or independence of the ideas on the theological strand or on any other strand of the Christian tradition. Let it be granted that Judaistic monotheism, in its conception of God as the supreme judge of men, is the historical root of the idea of the moral law. It does not follow that a modern conception of natural law cannot rest equally well on the pre-Christian Platonic theory of Forms, or on the naturalistic psychology of the Enlightenment. Let it be granted that the doctrines of the creation, the fall of man, and the redemption of man by Christ are the historical vehicles of our sense of human potentiality, of human evil, and of the possibility of living our lives nevertheless. It does not follow that our working conception of conflict in the soul cannot be founded rather on Plato's operational definitions of the parts of the soul, sketched in the *Republic,* or on Freud's clinical explorations of repression. Actually, as these examples suggest, there has been a tendency in Christendom to neglect the historical role both of the ancient Greeks and of modern Greeks like Hobbes and Hume, and to suppose that anything current in the thirteenth or the eighteenth century derives from Christian doctrine. But if my tradition is Christian, and Socrates is part of my tradition, we understand well enough the sense in which that makes Socrates part of the Christian tradition. The reason I can accept most of the Thomist account of the human soul is that it is mainly Aristotelian, and I accept nearly all of Aristotle's account of soul. However, leaving aside historical questions, my present point is that even in those cases where we owe an idea uniquely to Christian insight, or to Jesus himself, the full assimilation of it into our own view of the world calls for ingratitude. Our attitude to our Chris-

tian heritage, as to our Greek heritage and our Chinese heritage, is properly exploitative.

How does the process of secular exploitation work? Let me
illustrate, with respect to Scott's account, first the identification of nontheological issues, then the kind of problem which
arises in characterizing the residue, and finally the secular attitude to doctrines held to be empty.

Much of the secularization of the Christian tradition is
naturally being accomplished by those Christian thinkers
who are, as Scott remarks, eager for a "dialogue with modern
man" (see p. 10), and who accordingly go as far as they can
to exhibit the content of their message in terms understood
by those lacking a theology. I suspect the danger they run
is not that of performing too "drastic a surgery on the Christian message," but that of discovering how much of what
they have to say can be successfully preserved. For to the
extent that they succeed in reaching the secular mind, theological references are shown to be the idiom rather than the
substance of at least that part of their belief.

Consider the familiar dialectic which Scott introduces between man's creation in the image of God and his fallen state.
On the one hand, there is "glory," and the possibility of living for other men; on the other hand, there is perversity, and
the injustice and self-centeredness of each self. "To speak
of the *originality* of his sin is to speak of its tragically disruptive presence in every moment of experience . . ." (see
pp. 14-15). Now the critical question, in which we are all involved, is that of the nature of our defect. In the name of
Christian anthropology Scott rejects any explanation by
biological determinants residing in our animal nature. He
rejects social and historical determinants, and in general
rejects any explanation by reference to empirical facts as

being deterministic, and incompatible with freedom and responsibility. He rejects the Socratic diagnosis of ignorance. In short he reaffirms the classical ascription to the human exercise of free will. However, he also regards man as "flawed" by his own perversity, and thereby rendered, apparently, "incapable of delivering himself from his deepest woe" (see pp. 15-16).

This combination of responsibility for our evil, and inability to escape it, whereby a sort of moral determinism appears to entrap us where all other determinisms have failed, is I suppose characteristically a traditional Christian view. At the same time it is statable, as it has just been stated, in nontheological terms. It is interesting that the same problem attends one of the most striking secular attacks on determinism. One of the enterprises Sartre most pursues throughout his works is to rescue the empirical discoveries of Marx and Freud from their respective forms of determinism. His own intransigent assertion of human freedom and responsibility is carried so far that it threatens to preclude any account of the stability and uniformity actually found in human conduct. His appeal from a given human nature, which he denies, to the human condition, which we share, does not solve the problem of the difficulty which an individual has to recast his way of life, or the problem of the nature of the bewitchments into which, as Sartre admits, human consciousness is able to fall. My point here is not to explore these problems; it is to show how familiar the issues are in strictly secular terms. The main difference between the Christian view which Scott expounds, and the view of *L'être et le néant,* which he cites for nihilistic bleakness, is that the Sartrean view maintains the inalienable possibility of delivering ourselves from our own perversity by the exercise

of our freedom. Both the existentialist and the Christian re-
affirmations of freedom contribute usefully to the re-examination of determinism—and of the great classical problems
in secular philosophy that of freedom and determinism is
perhaps the center once again of the study of human nature.

The question to be examined is this: What has been left
out of the doctrines of the creation, the fall, and the moral
attributes of God, in a version which embodies only their
contribution to this secular debate? In particular, does the
mention of God add anything to this version of the Christian conception *of man?*

It would be reasonable to suggest that much turns on the
assertion that our nature is in the image of God's, and to
suggest that the content of this assertion is given by another: that God has revealed himself in history. Once again,
however, our question requires us to sift out the elements
which are common property to begin with. That the life of
Jesus was a revelation of the possibilities of human beings,
that it revealed what integrity of character and clarity of
mind can be like when animated by love—this is not Christian doctrine. It is ordinary psychological and moral reflection on historical fact. What confronts the secular person is
rather the doctrine that the life of Jesus was a revelation of
God. One form of our question could be just this: What is
the difference between saying that that life was a revelation,
and saying that it was a revelation of God?

In this process, often repeated, I find myself brought as a
secular person to the problem of what to make of *pure
theology.* I do make something of it, and it would be
philistine to deny its interest. What I make of it is myth and
poetry. This is one way to take it seriously, and the greatness of myth and poetry is the measure of the nourishment
one stands to gain from them. But the condition is not at-

tached that one must believe them to consist of true propositions. It is also appropriate to set one myth against another, and to deny to any poetic vision exclusive power over one's imagination.

Naturally, therefore, this grant of status as myth and poetry, while offered as a concession, will be received without enthusiasm. Though not the crudest form of rationalist dismissal, it evidently turns aside the believer's claim to be putting forward a doctrine which is true, which might have been false, and about which he feels that its being true rather than false is the most important thing to be known about the world. Once this claim is lost, the positive account of the theological residue is of relatively academic interest. Belief in the existence of God is after all the heart of the matter, and it seems to me that the constant tendency of modern reflection on this doctrine is to show that, to the extent that one insists on giving it the status of a true proposition, it is an empty proposition. I do not mean that the believer and nonbeliever have come to understand the proposition differently, so that it has content for the one but is empty for the other. I mean that, according to the nonbeliever, the believer misconceives the status of his own doctrine, mistakes the interpretations of a myth for the implications of a fact, and thereby fails to realize that his own doctrine is empty.

This is to describe the limit toward which belief in God is approximating. It would oversimplify the dialectic to suggest that this had always been the condition of Christian belief; and since many of its historical forms survive abundantly, it would oversimplify the contemporary scene to suggest that so much as a majority of Christians have reached this stage. In past struggles believers have defended their cosmology, or their geology, or their psychology, or their theory of history as an integral part of their belief about God. Later believers have had the task of dissociating their faith from any claim over these lost battlefields. They have usually argued that it was a misunderstanding of their essential beliefs to try to deduce such consequences from them. In fact, I think that many past believers, and many present believers, do not so much draw illegitimate consequences from belief in God as hold a different belief, rich indeed in content, expressed in the same form of words; the sophisticated believer has actually reinterpreted the ancient formula and *come* to hold a belief lacking this content.

Where substantial consequences really flow from theological doctrines that have been held or are still held, and where this content has not previously been obtained from some empirical source, I will say roundly that all such consequences either are demonstrably false or quite lack corroboration or support. On that level we do have head-on conflicts between Christian doctrine and the empirical disciplines, including the empirical studies of human nature. Then the secular challenge is scientific rather than philosophical. My contention is only that if we follow the reinterpretation of theological doctrine, and allow its most sophisticated contemporary forms to speak for it, a limit of vacuousness is approached. Not only is the appropriate critique then nonempirical, and conceptual, the doctrine itself has adopted a philosophical principle to govern its own interpretation. This principle is stated as the final abandonment of natural theology. From there it is a philosophical task to show that the impossibility in principle of a natural theology entails the vacuousness of theological doctrine.

To carry out, or merely to sketch, this philosophical task would require another essay. In place of the account itself, let me offer a historical identification of the line of thought. The logical positivists tried to make short execution of theology by dogmatic application of the principle of verification. This attempt can be agreed to have been crude in logic and philistine in spirit, and the corresponding attempt in ethics no longer needs to be taken seriously. But with respect to theology, the substance of this enterprise had a powerful and subtle precedent in Hume's *Dialogues Concerning Natural Religion,* and the subsequent analytic tradition in English-speaking philosophy has refined and developed a fundamentally positivist approach to theological doctrine. This approach retains its power as long as the believer claims to say something about what really exists or does not exist. For it is precisely by that claim that he submits himself to the ordinary standards for the intelligible assertion of truths. Nor does the philosopher's failure to understand wear, I feel, the familiar air of theoretical commitment or deduction from prejudice. It recalls rather this moment:

QUEEN: To whom do you speak this?
HAMLET: Do you see nothing there?
QUEEN: Nothing at all, yet all that is I see.

The philosopher is similarly offering, as I read him, not a dogmatic denial, but a faithful report of his experience.

What Is the Relevance of Scientific Explanation?

The second issue I have undertaken to examine is raised by the realization that the secular view of human nature is not set in opposition to any irreducibly Christian view of human nature, and that the irreducibly Christian theological doctrines are set in opposition to a philosophical critique and not to the secular view of human nature. On neither ground, apparently, can we explain why the modern empirical accounts of human nature seem powerfully relevant to Christian belief, no matter how sophisticated its form.

I have said that ambivalence about the bearing of empirical explanation on rational criticism is now widespread. I believe that the problem we have in understanding this bearing is due to a lack in the contemporary philosophy of human nature. What is needed is a modern account of the sense in which man is a rational animal. There are historical reasons why the theory of rationality should have fallen into neglect, especially in the English tradition, and the very existence of the topic needs to be recalled. This must be my excuse for some general remarks about it.

Let us like good Aristotelians speak of the soul of an organism as consisting of those faculties which it has in virtue of its organic structure, and let us speak freely of organisms, including people, as having the faculty of doing anything which they can in fact do. We are thereby allowed to distinguish as many faculties, from excretion to hearing to mathematical intuition, as will serve to provide working classifications of the things people can do. There is an old tradition which favors a classification into intellect, emotion, and will.

If we survey the thoughts, feelings, and actions of men, and try to make them intelligible, we may be struck by a systematic difference between men and the other animals which also think, feel, and act. In trying to explain why men think, feel, and act as they do, we find that they do these things for reasons. To understand the reasons a man has for thinking as he does, or feeling as he does, or acting as he does, is very often to have the relevant and complete explanation of why he does. Still oftener, perhaps, when he is being less than perfectly rational, the indispensable route to understanding him is to plot the angle and distance of his deflection from what there was *reason* to think, to feel, or to do in his situation. In short, the things a man does become intelligible only when we take into account another, higher-order, pervasive faculty which he has. He is able not merely to believe something, fear something, or make something happen, but to do so for a reason. This ability is the faculty of reason, and by having it we are rational as opposed to nonrational creatures. Its function is regulative, and when we are so regulated we are rational as opposed to irrational.

It needs saying to the contemporary psychologist and sociologist that this conception of men as organisms possessing the faculty of reason is the ordering principle of the kind of explanation of human thought, feeling, and action on which we have always depended, and on which we still mainly depend. To the extent that this kind of explanation is possible the lives of individual people are in principle mutually intelligible. It proceeds by approximations to a rational reconstruction of another's mind, looking at his situation from his point of view. It must therefore be contrasted with what is called scientific explanation, and in particular with causal explanation. The essential feature of scientific explanation is to bring the thing explained under laws of nature, in the sense of inductive or empirical regularities observed from a spectator's point of view.

A psychologist may suppose, what his title implies, that his discipline is to give the whole account of the soul—that it just is the study of human nature. He may also assume nowadays that it is an empirical science, whose results must consist of inductively established laws. Yet these two easy assumptions, working together, will fatally constrict his view. He will look for causal explanations of everything human, and may end by confining his attention to those low-level or abnormal phenomena where such explanations have been found. He will miss the only kind of explanation which has ever succeeded with human activities of intellectual and moral interest, since these call for reconstruction from the point of view of a fellow rational being.

The problem of free will has a central position nowadays because it is the conceptual turbulence made by the confluence, in the area of action, of these two main kinds of explanation. The conditions of straightforward rational reconstruction of the agent's mind are, in the case of conduct, what we call the conditions for moral responsibility. It is their presence which it proves difficult to reconcile with the possibility of causal explanation. For determinism very plausibly asserts this possibility in every case, even though the possibility has never been fulfilled in any actual case of responsible human action.

Belief is very different from will. But it is equally a human faculty regulated by reason, and one advantage of a general account of rationality is to bring out parallel problems in explaining belief, including religious belief, by rational reconstruction and by causal explanation. Let me now apply to the case of belief certain general remarks about the relation between the two kinds of explanation.

Pure examples of the two kinds are mutually exclusive. If someone believes what he believes because there are good reasons for believing it, that stands as the explanation of why he does, and the question of the cause of his belief does not arise. Justification and explanation coincide. The question of cause arises only when reasons are lacking, when not even a person's mistakes or ignorance or limitations of point of view will help us to follow his thinking, and we confess the opaqueness of his state of mind by an ascription of irrationality. Conversely, where we can locate the cause of a man's belief in conditioning, or drug action, or powerful anxiety, that belief will cease to be something to which his reasoning processes are relevant. Nor can we intelligibly debate its merits with him, or regard his mind as in that respect sane and normal. It is a presupposition of our ordinary discussions with each other that we lack a scientific explanation of each other's beliefs.

It does not matter here whether this incompatibility is necessary, or whether it is due to the crudity of our empirical psychology and physiology. Grant for the moment that only the unimaginable complexity of the structure of the brain prevents us from giving the causes of our most rational beliefs. It would still be a fact that any cause now known is so simple as to guarantee a level of mental functioning far below that of the rational human being.

What are the practical consequences for inquiry and debate? I think they are, first, that rational justification takes priority over causal explanation, and second, that apparent causal explanation of a belief calls for a skeptical re-examination of its justification. Freud says, for example: ". . . in past times religious ideas, in spite of their incontrovertible lack of authentication, have exercised the strongest possible influence on mankind. This is a fresh psychological problem. We must ask where the inner force of those doctrines lies and to what it is that they owe their efficacy, independent as it is of recognition by reason." [1] Such an introduction to a theory of religious beliefs as wish-fulfillments implies that the theory would not be in order without a prior judgment that the beliefs lacked the support of reason. By implication Freud is admitting that the occasion for his psychological inquiry is generated by independent conclusions, for which he accepts responsibility, on the merits of the beliefs. Conversely, if a believer is confronted with an alleged psychoanalytic explanation of his belief, and this explanation looks plausible, he has a problem. Since the explanation presupposes the lack of justification of his belief, there must be something wrong with one or the other. Certainly he will examine the explanation with skepticism, but he will also be obliged to a skeptical re-examination of the grounds for his own religious belief. If he is led by this new rational inquiry to abandon the belief, then the psychological account is ready made to complete the picture.

The application of these precepts to demonstrably false doctrines is obvious enough. My thesis has been, however, that the believer tends more and more to reinterpretations which achieve security from refutation at the price of saying nothing refutable, and finally of saying nothing at all. The irrationality for which we might seek empirical explanations is therefore subtle. It consists in attaching enormous importance to propositions for which no content can be found, or in regarding as profoundly significant experiences whose significance cannot be conveyed. Such forms of belief in God or experience of God have analogues in other fields of discussion, for example assertions of self-evidence in mathematics. For all such cases defense on a rational plane is naturally conceived on the model of perception: it just *appears* to one to be so. Such appeals might after all be appropriate; they cannot be avoided at some stage in any inquiry. But their freedom from intellectual difficulty depends on their appearing so to others as well.

Once disagreement has rendered a matter problematic, the relation between the two types of explanation may be implicitly recognized in the question: *Why* should it seem to many people to be so, unless they are endowed with the capacity to see or feel that it is? Even at this stage, it might be possible to defend the claims of a special religious susceptibility, or of a

kind of experience which others in perversity deny to themselves. As long as the question is unanswerable, it can be asked
rhetorically, and sheer testimony is left in the field. But then
an actual answer from psychology or sociology is correspond-
ingly deflating.

In my own judgment, the matter is more than problematic.
The believer seems to me to be caught by a dilemma of falsity
or vacuousness, according to his interpretation of theological
doctrines. In either event, the gates are open to the full current of the empirical understanding of religious phenomena.
The psychoanalytic interpretation of theological symbolism,
the class analysis of denominational adherence, the compara-
tive history of movements, the surveying of variation in ideological attitudes—there is no limit to the material now admitted to relevance. We feel its force not primarily because
it conflicts with any uniquely Christian conception of man,
but because it comes upon us through this channel which, if
not explicitly thought, is often obscurely felt to be open;
namely, the antecedent loss in the central Christian doctrines
either of plausibility or of content.

Having presented my two theses with less diffidence than
the darkness of these matters might seem to call for, I must be
allowed a few disclaimers. In defending the conception of
man as a creature with rational nature, I make no comment
on the degree of irrationality of our past or present perform-
ance. The starkest account of human barbarity and self-de-
structiveness can be expressed in these very terms. Nor do I
imply that no other features of our nature, besides our reason, are uniquely human or uniquely valuable. In neither of
these ways do I feel committed to the shallow optimism or
the shallow intellectualism which one associates with nineteenth-century rationalist thought. But neither can I pretend

that in the middle of this century there exists a secular philosophy of human nature capable of sorting out the jumble of empirical knowledge we have about ourselves. If I somewhat elaborated my view of explanation by rational reconstruction it was with the secondary purpose of suggesting how radically we may have to revise our conception of psychology and the social sciences. Everything remains to be done. I look myself to Christian believers for guidance only as I do to a dozen sources, but in our philosophical condition we can be thankful for light from that direction as well.

6

Teilhard's Vision of Hope

by Pieter de Jong

In 1926, after attending a gathering where a Harvard professor had explained his views on the dawn of thought in the evolutionary process, Teilhard wrote:

I couldn't help thinking of the abyss that divides the intellectual world I was in and whose language I knew, from the theological world of Rome with whose idiom I am also familiar. At first it was something of a shock to realize that the latter could be, and indeed must be, just as real as the former; and then I told myself that now perhaps I was capable of so using the first language as to make it fairly express what the other contains but puts into words that most people can no longer understand.[1]

In these few words we have an outline of the work and life of Pierre Teilhard de Chardin. Immersed in his work and research he wanted to keep his faith. He loved the world but did not want to give up God. He became painfully aware that to the majority of people God and the world exclude each other. He also realized that the love of God is often expressed in a language which has lost its appeal to those who are engaged in the task of working with the things of the world. As a result the Church cannot communicate with the world. Humanity seems split between "religious" and "worldly" people. Actually the conflict is not so much between people as within individuals themselves who are torn between their love for

God and their love for the world. Around us and within us we see a lack of wholeness.

From Dividedness to Wholeness

Let us listen to Teilhard as he describes the various ways in which this conflict can hamper people's lives. In reading these words we discover that he is not describing others in a detached and objective manner. They represent stages of his own life, the temptation of which he has felt and fought and finally overcome.

There are first of all what he calls the distorted ones.[2] Many of them are found among the clergy and the followers of monastic orders. We also meet them among the laity. They have repressed their taste for the tangible and try to lead purely religious lives. They have said farewell to the world and withdrawn into some false kind of spirituality. They actually deny the goodness of God's creation and identify the negative forces of evil at work in the world with the world itself. They arrange for themselves a kind of world in which they have banished the largest possible number of earthly objects. They are distorted because they are not true to their own nature. They forget that even the making of such a choice presupposes their roots in the world of matter, and they will not succeed in finding God in the world. They are "otherworldly." Looking upon this false solution, he meditates:

But what would our spirits be, O God, if they did not have the bread of earthly things to nourish them, the wine of created beauties to intoxicate them, and the conflicts of human life to fortify them? What feeble powers and bloodless hearts Your creatures would bring You if they were to succeed in cutting themselves off prematurely from the providential setting in which You have placed them![3]

In the second place there are the disgusted ones. They have taken the opposite step. Having found out that the conflict between God and the world does not make sense and ruins their lives they have abandoned God. Instead of setting their affections on the things of the Spirit they devote themselves wholeheartedly to the things of this world and decide "to lead what seems to them a complete and human life." Using the terminology of Paul Tillich they have turned a preliminary concern into an ultimate one, and as a result their lives have become idolatrous. The question as to how things work has become everything to them. They no longer ask: "Why?" "Whence?" or "For what purpose?" The dimension of depth is gone from their lives. Teilhard was constantly aware of this threat to the person who becomes really involved in his work in the world, and he prays:

O God, whose call precedes the very first of our movements, grant me the desire to desire being—that, by means of that divine thirst which is Your gift, the access to the great waters may open wide within me. Do not deprive me of the sacred taste for being, that primordial energy, that very first of our points of rest. . . .
. . . grant that, after having desired, I may believe, and believe ardently and above all things, in Your active Presence.[4]

The majority of people in the Church, however, experience the conflict in a different manner. They have given up trying to make sense of the situation and lead a double life. They "never belong wholly to God, nor ever wholly to things." They are the divided ones who in some way admire both the distorted and the disgusted ones but do not have the courage to follow either stand completely. To these people the language of the Church and its rituals mean something, since they have grown up with them. Most of their time, however, they spend outside the Church, in labor or research, in routine or creative work. Here they experience the need to give themselves to the world. At the same time they do not want to give up God, and consequently their faith in God and their faithfulness to the world are two separate compartments. The more sensitive ones feel guilty that they cannot pursue God all the time. But the majority tend to be overwhelmed by the beauty and fascination of the world, as Teilhard well knew. If there is no positive relationship between God and the world the world will win:

> Disperse, O Jesus, the clouds with Your lightning! Show Yourself to us as the Mighty, the Radiant, the Risen! Come to us once again as the Pantocrator who filled the solitude of the cupolas in the ancient basilicas! Nothing less than this Parousia is needed to counter-balance and dominate in our hearts the glory of the world that is coming into view. And so that we should triumph over the world with You, come to us clothed in the glory of the world.[5]

Having faced and rejected the way of distortion or denial of the world, and of disgust or yielding to the world as ultimate reality, Teilhard overcame his dividedness by finding God in and through the world. "Diaphany" is one of his favorite words, which he uses to express that the world— not only the world of human relationships but the entire world of God's creation, including the realm of matter—becomes transparent to God for him who has the eyes to see. Teilhard does not try to argue us into faith. He, rather, presents a vision of the world and of man which is purely scientific or phenomenological, as he calls it, but which points beyond itself.

On the one hand, he wants to show that modern man does not have to bring a sacrifice of intellect or devotion to his task if he wants to believe in God and adore him. On the other hand, he is quite well aware that in order to share his entire vision man needs more than scientific training and intellectual acumen. He needs the Spirit of God himself who alone can bring about the diaphany.

Domine, fac ut videam. Lord, we know and feel that You are everywhere around us; but it seems that there is a veil before our eyes. *Illumina vultum tuum super nos*—let the light of Your countenance shine upon us in its universality. *Sit splendor Domini nostri super nos*—may Your deep brilliance light up the innermost parts of the massive obscurities in which we move. And to that end, send us Your Spirit, *Spiritus principalis,* whose flaming action alone can operate the birth and achievement of the great metamorphosis which sums up all inward perfection and towards which Your creation yearns: . . .[6]

Through his upbringing, character, and temperament Teilhard seemed destined for the struggle to find unity and wholeness. Born in France, in 1881, he was raised in a home where his mother instilled into him a profound devotion to God, and his father gave him a healthy appreciation for the concerns of everyday life. The boy who as a child had hidden his "gods" of iron and stone in his nursery, and who had been shocked at the discovery that even such solid objects were perishable, learned to search for the one and only Absolute.

As a Jesuit novice he was introduced to the spiritual exercises prescribed by Ignatius of Loyola and exposed to the theology of the Roman Catholic Church. At the same time he was trained in the disciplines of geology and, later on, of paleontology. Torn by what at that time seemed to him opposing loyalties he once almost gave up his desire to become a scientist, but the capable advice of his master and counselor guided him so that he continued his scientific career.[7] The result was a life dedicated to the service of God through engagement in the world.

Gradually, in his life and thought, the world and God are

knit together. The scientist who in his student days had been deeply influenced by Thomas à Kempis' *Imitatio*, and been inclined to look upon life as a matter of either/or, as a choice between work or contemplation, involvement or renunciation, found the key to a new kind of ascetic life. By ascetic he does not mean a training in the surrender of the world, but rather a discipline in accepting and shaping the world of God's creation and of resisting the forces which rend it apart and reduce it to the level of multiplicity.

Man, according to Teilhard, is called to working and suffering. In the past the Christian faith has laid most emphasis on the latter. It has gone into extremes to point out the darker aspects of life and the physical pains which Christ suffered. "You look at the crucifix from the wrong side," he said to his sister Françoise while she was undergoing a rigid period of testing before being admitted to the order of the Petites-Soeurs des Pauvres. "You should not only look at the cross; Jesus is on it!" [8]

In a world come of age, Teilhard wrote in 1926, we must discover that there is a great deal of truth in man's fashioning his own life and world.[9] The relevance of the Christian faith is not primarily in times of adversity, and the character of the Christian life is not predominantly that of resignation to pain, evil, and injustice. Man has been called to be God's co-creator. Therefore God is glorified in our active as well as in our passive life. A doctrine of work unfolds itself which gives new meaning to the ministry of the laity, consisting of work and service in the world. With man the evolutionary process has entered into a new stage. No longer does it continue as a blind force, but its progress or regress has been given into man's hands. Upon man's use of his God-given capacities the survival of this planet will depend. God is found in our active life. Like Bonhoeffer, Teilhard pleads for a knowledge of God not on the fringes of life, but in the center, in the things we know as well as those we do not know.[10]

With regard to suffering, even there a Christian is called to be active and resistant in the manner of Christ. Resignation does not come first but second. Resignation in the sense of fatalism is a pagan rather than a Christian virtue. Christian resignation is demanded but it does not absolve us from faithfulness to God and his world. The passive and the active life are closely interwoven and resignation "coincides with the maximum of fidelity to the human task." [11]

A new wholeness is born in which things that formerly appeared to be opposites are united as the two faces of one coin: achievement and suffering; engagement and detachment; work and worship; faith and science; spirit and matter; God and the world. They are brought together in a vision which gives harmony and new impetus to life in an age of estrangement.

From Dualism to Monism

The most common distinction we make when talking about man is that between body and soul. Our whole life is pervaded by it and our everyday language presupposes this duality. It has become so much part of our lives that we we have considerable difficulty entering into the world of those who did not use the distinction, e.g., in studying the language of primitive tribes or of the Old Testament.

Most people think of man in terms of a higher and a lower level. The body they regard as part of the world of nature, but the soul they consider of a higher order. The body is doomed to die, but the soul has an eternal destiny.

The official doctrine which hails from Descartes, is something like this. With the doubtful exceptions of idiots and infants in arms every human being has both a body and a mind. Some would prefer to say that every human being is both a body and a mind. His body and his mind are harnessed together, but after the death of the body his mind may continue to exist and function.[12]

Dualism between body and mind is so widespread in the Christian Church that many Christians are surprised when they learn that the Hebrews did not have words which are equivalent for "soul" and "body." We have read our dualism into the biblical writings. As a result many assert that the first chapters of Genesis teach it. Interpreting Gen. 2:7 they understand the words to mean: ". . . then the Lord God formed man of the dust from the ground, and breathed into his nostrils the breath of life; and he received a living soul." Actually the words read: ". . . then the Lord God formed man of the dust from the ground, and breathed into his nostrils the breath of life; and man became a living soul-being." The Hebrew word for "soul" does not indicate a part of man or a constituent of human nature. It indicates the whole man regarded from a specific point of view. The word which comes closest to our word "body" literally means "flesh" and it indicates the whole man considered as a perishable creature. "All flesh is grass" says the prophet (Isa. 40:6).

If we interpret Gen. 2:7 in a dualistic manner, man receives his soul from God as a divine spark. But if we are faithful to Hebrew thought we take these words to mean that by God's breath or creative power man is called to life. We are called into being by the Word of God and placed in a unique relationship with him which we can never make undone even if we deny it. The breath of God gives life to man and beast (cf. Gen. 7:22) and to the entire creation (Ps. 104:30). If God withholds his breath, man dies (Ps. 104: 29; Job 34:14). Man is not inherently immortal according to this view. If he dies the whole man dies. The Old Testament takes death seriously (cf. Isa., chap. 38, the Song of Hezekiah). The only hope for immortality would be if God continued to address man beyond death, but this possibility is hardly realized in the Old Testament.

The good news of Christ's life, death, and resurrection was preached in a world dominated by Hellenistic thought. It is not surprising that in such an environment soon the resurrection was confused with Plato's teaching on the immortality of the soul. Actually the resurrection is something quite different. Socrates died calmly believing that through death his soul finally was set free from bondage to his mortal body and could return to its divine origin. Christ, however, underwent the agony of death in the garden and on the cross and his disciples gave up hope when he lay in the tomb (Luke 24:21). The resurrection can only be seen as God's answer to Christ's life. He brought Jesus' whole life to fulfillment. Resurrection therefore is more than the survival of a part of man. The crucial difference between immortality of the soul and resurrection led the author of II Timothy (1:10) to say that Jesus Christ "abolished death and brought life and immortality to light through the gospel."

The monistic view of the Old Testament also colors the New. A striking example of Hebrew influence is the way in which Paul describes the resurrection body in I Cor. 15:44. He speaks of a "spiritual body." In a dualistic view this cannot be anything but a contradiction in terms. At the most it can mean a body as perfect tool of the spirit, but even this interpretation is basically dualistic. The expression can make sense only if the spiritual existence of the risen man is the fulfillment of his life in the body and thus a new kind of "body."

The word "monism," however, is liable to be misunderstood. This is particularly so if we adhere to a static view of man. There have been monistic interpretations of man within a static outlook, and they have meant the denial of either the material or the spiritual. Man then is either identified with the life of his psyche, and the realm of matter is reduced to the imagination, in which case spiritualism is the result (as with Berkeley who taught that all existence is really existence in the mind). Or man turns materialist and denies the realm of the spirit. Thought, then, is merely an activity of the brain, and man, as Feuerbach said, is what he eats.

Teilhard's monism is of a different kind. Instead of being static, it is dynamic. It does not deny the realm of matter or the realm of spirit. Whereas in static monism reality must be forced into one category, in dynamic monism matter and spirit are phases of one and the same world-stuff. In this view it is possible to take seriously both the world of matter and the importance of spirit. Matter and spirit become stages on the way in the development of the whole of reality.

By education and religion I had always admitted in a docile way that there is a basic heterogeneity between matter and spirit —body and mind, conscious and unconscious: two substances of a different nature, two species of being, incomprehensibly associated in the living composite, and of these one had to maintain at any price that the former was but the humble servant (not to say the opposite) of the latter. . . . Judge now my inward experience of liberation and joy when, at my first steps in an evolving universe, I discovered that the dualism in which one had held me so far, disappeared as a mist before the rising sun. Matter and spirit, not two things—but two states, two faces, of one and the same cosmic stuff, depending on the way you look at it, either extending it in the way in which it makes itself, or, on the contrary, in the way it gets lost.[13]

If spirit and matter are two phases of one world-stuff, the question arises as to how precisely these stages succeed one another. In order to understand Teilhard on this point we must have a closer look at his total world-view.

The history of the world is marked by three clearly distinguished phases: matter, life, and spirit. When the crust of the earth was sufficiently cooled off, there was the world of inorganic matter. At one time we spoke of this as "mere" matter but such a manner of speech indicates that we do not look at the entire thing. For Teilhard matter is not merely object but in some way also subject. It not only has an outside but also an inside. The atom is held together by forces from without and from within. Matter for Teilhard has a soul, or rather the potentiality of a soul.

At this early stage of the evolutionary process spirit was as it were dormant. The tangential energy or the forces that work on the without of things seem to dominate the course. The radial energy or the force which drives from within is hardly noticeable. Yet it is there, and it is one of the serious mistakes of science, according to Teilhard, that it has been merely concerned with what appears on the outside, with matter as object only.

Actually this world of matter, or geosphere, was far from passive or dead. It was continually preparing itself and being prepared for a new stage in the process. The geosphere can be compared with one of the inside rings on a tree trunk. The earth was becoming ripe to become covered with another layer:

Through a duration to which we can give no definite measure but know to be immense, the earth, cool enough now to allow the formation on its surface of the chains of molecules of the carbon type, was probably covered by a layer of water from which emerged the first traces of future continents. To an observer, equipped with even the most modern instruments of research, our earth would probably have seemed an inanimate desert. . . .

Then at a given moment, after a sufficient lapse of time, those same waters here and there must unquestionably have begun writhing with minute creatures. And from that initial proliferation stemmed the amazing profusion of organic matter whose matted complexity came to form the last (or rather the last but one) of the envelopes of our planet: the *biosphere*.[14]

The living cell is born, and the biosphere develops from the life of the virus to that of the plant and that of the animal world. Life is born of matter and yet it is something quite new. A threshold has been passed. And now we see even more clearly than before that a definite law is at work in the process of development. It is the law of increasing complexity and corresponding growth of consciousness. Whereas spirit had been expressed in the geosphere, or the realm of matter, on a level which suited that particular phase, now we see the emergence of a psychic aspect of life which is more complicated. Dogs can be trained and we say of them that they know their masters. Their soul life, however, remains on the level of the instinct. They do not yet know that they know.

Thus the biosphere prepares itself and is being prepared for another leap. The nervous system in certain branches of animal life grows more and more complex. The world is ripening for the dawn of another era, the life of man.

. . . if the mammals form a dominant branch, *the* dominant branch of the tree of life, the primates (i.e. those that are the cerebro-mammals) are its leading shoot and the anthropoids are the bud in which this shoot ends up.

Thenceforward, it may be added, it is easy to decide where to look in all the biosphere to see signs of what is to be expected. We already knew that everywhere the active phyletic lines grow warm with consciousness towards the summit. But in one well-marked region at the heart of the mammals, where the most powerful brains ever made by nature are to be found, they become red hot. And right at the heart of that glow burns a point of incandescence.

We must not lose sight of that line crimsoned by the dawn. After thousands of years rising below the horizon, a flame bursts forth at a strictly localised point.

Thought is born.[15]

With the birth of man the earth is being covered by another layer, the noosphere. At this stage of evolution spirit reaches the level of consciousness and the process of development takes on a new character. Whereas in the past evolution seemed to have been a product of outside forces—although as we have seen this is not altogether true because of the role of radial energy—now, with the birth of man, the process begins to determine itself. The birth of consciousness means the birth of freedom and responsibility. In man the evolutionary process has become conscious of itself. From now on spirit takes the lead and fulfills the preceding stages of life and matter. The process of spiritualization in him reaches a culmination point, but it is not yet finished. Man is not a finished product and the process of noogenesis goes on. From now on the changes will be more inward, in the life of the mind rather than in outward appearance. Increasing complexity will lead to increasing consciousness on the part of all human beings.

This is Teilhard's monism. It is a monism of world-stuff, not a monism which cancels the difference between the Creator and the creature. To Teilhard spirit and Spirit are qualitatively different even if at some stage of his development he was drawn toward pantheism. It is a monism which does not allow for speculations regarding the origin of the soul apart from the ground in which man is rooted. He does not deny the creation of the soul, but the word "creation" must be understood in such a way that God is present in the process which leads to the birth of consciousness. Science, so far, has never taken the trouble, he claims, to look at the whole man. And theology has refused to take seriously man's being interwoven with the entire creation. We do not glorify God by saying, "Trailing clouds of glory do we come," if we mean by these words that the soul comes directly from God (see above, pp. 10-11). The glorious character of man appears when we learn to see in him the key to our understanding of the universe. Not only scientifically, but also theologically speaking, new horizons are opened up if we follow Teilhard's lead in this matter.

From a Static to a Dynamic View

Today we frequently hear about man's loss of nerve and self-confidence. Part of the reason undoubtedly is the way in which during the ongoing centuries man has been pushed from the center of the universe to the fringes. In primitive world-views man was regarded as the center of the earth and the earth was the center of the universe. This was particularly so when the earth was thought of as a flat pancake, but it was still true in the Ptolemaic world-view in which the earth was considered round. There was a remarkable coincidence in this world-view between space and meaning. Professor John Dillenberger says of it:

The general picture of the universe was clear. At its centre was the immobile planet—Earth. It was composed of earth and water, the two lowest of the four elements. Hell was at the centre of the earth and at the greatest distance from the heavens. The abandoning of the notion of a flat earth resulted in certain modifications, but the conception of the world was not basically altered. The worldpicture was still essentially hierarchical in the spatial as well as in the philosophical and theological sense. Such a world could be visualized. Its meaning could also be discerned. Space and destiny coincided in this world that so fruitfully mixed Ptolemaic, Aristotelian and Biblical assumptions. The whole universe ministered to the earth, and the domain of nature assured the significance of man and of the drama of redemption.[16]

For ages the faith of the Church has been expressed in terms of this world-view. We can appreciate the shock which the Copernican revolution meant to people whose faith was bound to it. Man was no longer spatially the center of the universe, since the earth was just a planet off the center. It is amazing how the Church survived the shock. Man's superiority was maintained because of his being endowed with reason which came straight from God. Man's psyche became the center. From the Renaissance until the last century this attitude guaranteed some appreciation of man's significance. But it did not last beyond the middle of the nineteenth century. Man's kinship with the animal world, as described by Darwin, to many implied that he was nothing but an animal, and it seemed impossible to maintain that he was the crown of creation.

For Teilhard there is no reason to long for a restoration of the picture in which man is the spatial center of the universe. Our knowledge has recently gained revolutionary insights into the time dimension of the universe and our world. If we are willing to accept a dynamic instead of a static view, he claims, we shall see that man's crucial place in creation is regained in a totally different and even more impressive manner.

What is the difference between a static and a dynamic view of the universe?[17] In a static view things have been practically the same from the moment they were made until now. There have been no incisive changes, only ripples on the surface. The components of the universe were created separate "species" which are not related to each other. Man in this view is like a statue on a pedestal. The statue and the pedestal have nothing in common. The world is put together in the way of a machine. Because the dimension of time is lacking, all progress is relative and not very important.

In a dynamic view the creative function of time is realized. The world is not made as a finished product but develops as a creative process. The various components grow out of each other and are intimately related. Man, in this view, is like a flower on a plant: Just as a flower sums up the life of the root and the stem and the leaves, so man contains in himself all preceding stages of the evolutionary development and leads them to fulfillment. Because of the emphasis on time, history is of vital importance, and the universe is a vast and dynamic historical process.

We can hardly estimate the impact of this change in outlook upon our whole life. It certainly exceeds the effect of the Copernican revolution. Christians, according to Teilhard, should not repeat the mistakes of the days of Galileo but, rather, participate in this revolution, including their faith. The Christian faith has nothing to fear here as long as we are willing to look at the whole man and at the entire creation in this dynamic development. If we do so and also pay attention to the growth of spirit in the succeeding stages or spheres, man appears as the spearhead of the evolutionary process. In some way he is more central than ever before since in him the evolutionary process begins consciously to lead itself toward the goal.

It is striking how some ideas raised in the Old Testament and in the New, which hardly made sense in terms of a static

view, now come to life. One of them is the way in which the
fate of man decides the fate of the entire creation. Because of
sin the entire creation is held back (Gen. 3:17, 18). In the
redemption of man the whole creation participates (Isa. 11:
6 ff.; 65:17 ff.). We think of Rom. 8:19 ff., where creation is
pictured as groaning in travail to see the revelation of the
freedom of the sons of God. Man's cosmic significance is
fulfilled in the cosmic significance of the Christ. Teilhard
repeatedly quotes Col. 1:17, where we read that in Christ
"all things hold together." Teilhard's Christ is a cosmic
Christ. He sums up the history of the whole creation since
he "fills all in all" (Eph. 1:23).

It is not surprising that these ideas come to life in a
dynamic world-view. The biblical concept of redemptive
history, beginning with the call of Abraham who was set on
his way by God, and more fully expressed in the Exodus
where the people of God were given a new beginning, and
culminating in the resurrection of Christ as the beginning
of the new creation, has contributed to the rise of the dynamic empirical world-view of which we are speaking. In the
Bible, however, the dynamic view of redemption is somehow fitted into a static view of creation and the universe.
This has been even more so in the faith of the Church.
Today our eyes are opened to the way in which redemption
and creation are interwoven as we are led to a dynamic
understanding of creation as well.

We come back to the quotation from Teilhard's letter at
the beginning of this chapter. There he spoke of the break-
down of communication between the Church and the world,
because the language of the Church is so different from the
language of the world. "Translation" of the faith into the
language of our contemporary thought-world amounts to
more than here and there replacing an outmoded word or

expression by a modern one. It actually means translating the faith which has been expressed in terms of a static world-view into the language of an empirical, dynamic view. Here lies Teilhard's significance for theology. Not a theologian himself he has pointed theologians the way they must go in order to proclaim the gospel in a language which is not only comprehensible but also very well suited to the purpose of proclaiming God's great acts in creation and redemption.

Some of the implications of the change from a static to a dynamic world-view for theology we have already noticed in considering the nature of the soul of man. The dynamic view forbids us to accept an explanation which leaves out its origin in the prehuman stages of the evolutionary process.

We have also seen the implications for our picture of God. Whereas in a static view God is the God "above" who guides his creation by "remote control" in a deistic manner, in a dynamic view he is immanent in the process, yet not identical with it. While in a static view he appears predominantly at the beginning, in a dynamic view he is at the end drawing the development to a conclusion. For Teilhard, God is God "ahead." [18]

The change of world-view forces us to pay particular attention to those doctrines which have been traditionally called the doctrines of the beginning and the end, of creation and consummation. Creation, as we have seen with the origin of the world, does not mean that God directly brings about the finished product. In a static world-view creation is mainly a "big bang" at the beginning. In a dynamic view it is the creative process, implying a beginning. Evolution itself is not creative but evolution is the way in which creation takes place. In Teilhard's view creation means "letting things make themselves."

One of the areas where Christian theology is forced to do

a great deal of rethinking is the doctrine of original sin. It is not sufficient to say that the story of the Fall is a myth (see above, p. 14). Even as a myth it presupposes a static world-view in which man appears on the scene as a practically finished product. Not the mythological character of the story but this presupposition prevents the communication of the truth implied in the tale. In a static world-view the ideal is in the past, while in a dynamic view it lies in the future. In terms of a static view the third chapter of Genesis tells us that God is not the author of evil, that man is responsible for his failure, and that sin is a matter of the race and not of the individual alone.

In translating these truths into a dynamic world-view we must emphasize that man was not made a finished product, and that he is responsible for his falling short of the goal. We miss the mark (*hamartia*). In our missing the mark, however, we do not stand alone but are influenced by our past, background, and environment, and at the same time we prevent others and the rest of creation from attaining the goal. Saying No to the forward trend means that we hamper our own development and that of the entire creation of which we are a part and out of which we are born.

The change of world-view particularly influences our doctrine of eschatology or the consummation. In order to have a clearer idea of this we must have a look at Teilhard's view of the end.

From the Past to the Future

The more Teilhard learned from his examination of the past, the more he became interested in the future. In 1935 he wrote:

It is almost as though, for reasons arising from the progress of my own science, the past and its discovery had ceased to interest me. The past has revealed to me how the future is built and preoccupation with the future tends to sweep everything else aside.[19]

Interest in the future is another characteristic of Teilhard's phenomenology or "hyperphysics." He admits that a science of the future does not make statements with the same certainty as a science about the past. Yet he stresses that it presents something different from mere speculations. The term "hyperphysics" indicates that he wants to give a kind of outline—not in detail, of course—of the future, which is based on his observations of the past.

The future is of the greatest importance to man, and it is feasible, according to Teilhard, to begin with an examination of the present situation. Taking seriously the noogenesis (growing process of consciousness) going on in our days, we notice some interesting changes. As soon as man was born he began to populate the earth and spread himself over the globe. It was the era of expansion and of development of individual consciousness. Today, however, this period belongs to the past. Practically the whole earth is populated and people are brought into closer contact with each other than ever before. Outwardly they do not change very much but inwardly they go through a most important development. They are learning to think in cosmic terms.

The present trend became possible partly because of man's progress in science and technology. Modern means of communication bring him from one part of the globe to another within a few hours. Present-day migration contributes to an interchange of cultures. Radio and television provide us in our living rooms with descriptions and pictures of what goes on in the remotest parts of the world.

For Teilhard this is a sign that the law of increasing complexity and corresponding growth of consciousness is still at work, and he assumes that it will continue to work in the future. After the birth of man comes the birth of mankind.[20] Borderlines between nations and cultures are being effaced. Following a diverging trend exhibited by the human race in its earlier stages, now a converging pattern is beginning to show. Mankind is undergoing drastic changes in the sense of an increasing socialization. Human beings are finding out that they can no longer live in isolation. In order to become more fully man we must associate with others and live with them. Man is man with and for others. Our age gives not only an illustration of this trend but also of the struggles which accompany this process. Two world wars and the failure of the League of Nations are the "growing pains" of mankind on the way to unity.

We are mistaken if we think that the birth of the "ultra-human" as Teilhard calls it, is inevitable and guaranteed without any risks. Evolution at this level is not merely driven, but drives itself. Human freedom is a factor of the greatest importance and man can refuse the trend toward greater unity even if it means his self-destruction. The hazards increase with the potentialities. Thus the unification of the human race is not necessarily a step forward compared with the individualization which went on until a relatively short time ago. We are faced with the risk of massification.

Some, in reading these ideas of Teilhard, may have thought that he came very close to Karl Marx who also taught that the world was being prepared for unification and socialization. The unity of mankind, however, which Karl Marx expected is one in which the individual lives for the mass and loses his individuality. To Teilhard this would mean the loss of one of the most precious gains in the evolutionary process: individual consciousness. Teilhard's picture of so-

cialization is not that of the antheap or the beehive. Unification of the human mind to him implies an unfolding of the
human personality which comes to fulfillment in this "super-
consciousness" without loss of the self.

How does Teilhard avoid the loss of individuality in his
picture of the new consciousness? From what we have said
it is obvious that the evolutionary process for him is leading
to an end. He calls this the Omega-point. Omega is the goal
toward which creation moves and where all things and people finally will be united and made whole. Omega, however,
is much more than merely the end of the line. Since the
evolutionary process in its later stages is a conscious one, the
unity at the end must be a goal that can be desired and
loved. How else can Omega call forth the response of human
beings except if it is personal itself? This Omega-point to
Teilhard is the Christ who draws the whole of reality to
himself to fill it with his presence.

For the Christian, striving toward unity is a conscious
response to Christ's invitation:

No, You do not ask anything false or unattainable of me. You
merely, through Your revelation and Your grace, force what is
most human in me to become conscious of itself at last. Humanity
was sleeping—it is still sleeping—imprisoned in the narrow joys
of its little closed loves. A tremendous spiritual power is slumber-
ing in the depths of our multitude, which will manifest itself only
when we have learnt to break down the barriers of our egoisms
and, by a fundamental recasting of our outlook, raise ourselves
up to the habitual and practical vision of universal realities.

Jesus, Saviour of human activity to which You have given
meaning, Saviour of human suffering to which You have given
living value, be also the Saviour of human unity; compel us to
discard our pettinesses, and to venture forth, resting upon You,
into the uncharted ocean of charity.[21]

The Omega-point is ambiguous in the sense that, on the one hand, it is the center toward which all things tend, and on the other it transcends the development. Omega is prepared and at the same time goes beyond all preparation. Here lies the key to Teilhard's understanding of the relationship between history and its fulfillment.

In a static world-view the end is seen as a catastrophe. As a result the link between the consummation and history preceding it has been frequently neglected in the faith of the Church, except for the personal histories.[22] There are exceptions, like the optimistic approach which arose in the last century under the impact of the evolutionary world-view. Then history was practically identified by some with the coming of the Kingdom of God. Teilhard is kept from such an identification because his Omega-point shows both continuity and discontinuity, and both are taken seriously.

The fulfillment is discontinuous in the sense that even the universe, like the individual, has to go through a last sacrifice or death before it can become united with the personal center of the Christ. The pleroma at the end is a spiritual transformation. The fulfillment is continuous in the sense that it is being prepared in world history and that our attitude toward the end makes a difference. Christian hope is one of the essential virtues, and this hope is expressed in the actual engagement in the tasks of the world by which we prepare the coming of the end. Thus our work in the world receives meaning in the light of the end where it will be transformed (cf. I Cor. 15:58).

Teilhard draws a parallel between the Incarnation and the consummation. In both cases we can speak of a preparation and of a fulfillment which transcends the expectation.

One day, the Gospel tells us, the tension gradually accumulating between humanity and God will touch the limits prescribed by the possibilities of the world. And then will come the end. Then the presence of Christ, which has been silently accruing in things, will suddenly be revealed—like a flash of light from pole to pole.[23]

Here we also see the significance of the Church in Teilhard's thought. The Church is the place where the "Christification" of the world takes place. The Church is the Body of Christ through which Christ is present in the world of today and begins to fill all things. In the Eucharist the sacrifice of the whole world, of its accomplishments and pains is offered up to God on behalf of all, in expectation of the final sacrifice of the whole creation to God.[24]

We have called Teilhard's thoughts about man a vision of hope. Now we realize that this hope really is based on his faith that God finally will draw all men together into one and become all in all. Over and against the despair of our age he has presented a vision in which he starts with the phenomena as he empirically examines them. But at all points these phenomena point beyond themselves, toward the God in the future. His vision, therefore, is not an argument or proof for the existence of God. It is, rather, an effort to make us see that faith in God does not force us to give up faith in man or in the world. In the final analysis they cannot fail because they are God's creation.

The World Come of Age:
A Second Look at Bonhoeffer*

by Reginald H. Fuller

In sophisticated intellectualist Christian circles and, since the *Honest to God* debate, in the wider public, there has been much talk about a number of phrases coined by the late Dietrich Bonhoeffer, the German martyr who died in a concentration camp on April 9, 1945. Among these slogans is the concept of "the world come of age." Much has been written about it, and much of what has been written shows that Bonhoeffer's concept is being misunderstood and misused. There have been helpful attempts to clarify this and other popular Bonhoeffer phrases, notably in the German work of Bonhoeffer's editor, Eberhard Bethge[1] and in the pioneer study by John Godsey.[2] Both of these writers, in different ways, are concerned to demonstrate the unity of Bonhoeffer's thought throughout his life. Above all they seek to show that his latest thought (including the concept of a world come of age) represents no sudden novelty, but is the climax of his earlier thought. They seek to demonstrate that the latest thinking is rooted specifically in his Christological studies during the earliest period of his writing. The

* Page references preceded by *LP* in this chapter refer to Bonhoeffer, *Letters and Papers from Prison*, ed. by Eberhard Bethge and trans. by Reginald H. Fuller (London: S.C.M. Press, 1956).

reason for these studies has been partly defensive. Many critics, especially in Germany, have dismissed Bonhoeffer's latest thinking or have sought to explain it away, on the ground that in the terrible experience of the concentration camp he lost his faith, or at least his nerve. Even Karl Barth has taken this line. Bonhoeffer, he complains, was "an impulsive visionary thinker." He was always thinking up something new, coining a striking phrase for it, and then going off again at a tangent.* Bethge and Godsey have been concerned at all costs to persuade theology and the Church to take Bonhoeffer seriously. We have no desire to compete with their efforts. Instead, we propose here to undertake the more limited task of studying one of Bonhoeffer's concepts, that of the world's coming of age, in the context in which it was developed. We hope thereby to discover exactly what he did mean and what he did not mean by it. Only so will we be able to avert the misunderstandings, and discover both its value and its limitations for theology and the Church today.

Analysis of the Letters

In a series of letters to a friend—Eberhard Bethge—written from prison during the period from Nov. 20, 1943 to July 21, 1944 (*LP*, pp. 71-185) Bonhoeffer is reflecting on the situation which will face the German Church very shortly —soon after the collapse, which he knows is coming. Remember, Bonhoeffer had lived through the Church struggle before the war, and had been actually involved in the plot

---

* *Mündige Welt,* Vol. I, p. 121. *Mündige Welt* is a periodically published series devoted to the interpretation of Bonhoeffer's thought and including mainly, though not exclusively, papers read at a (usually) bi-annual conference held at Weissensee, Berlin. To date Vols. I-IV have appeared.

against Hitler. Remember too, that in prison, he found himself for the first time up against the products of the Third Reich and encountered secularists at close quarters. Hitherto his life had been a sheltered one, both ecclesiastical and academic. It was a shock to him to discover how far modern man was alienated from the Church and from all the traditions which he himself held so dear, the traditions of Bible, creed, and culture. And it led him to reflect on what all this might mean for a Christian. What does Christ mean in this situation? Who is he today? (*LP*, p. 121.)

The first few letters describe life in prison, and there is little intellectual reflection. His Bible and hymnal are Bonhoeffer's constant companions. He has adopted (Nov. 21) the long neglected advice of Luther to begin morning and evening prayers with the sign of the cross. But he is careful to explain: "I shan't come out of here a *homo religiosus*" (*LP*, p. 73). That is to say, he is not bent on cultivating an individualist piety or holiness. On the contrary, he has adopted the practice because "there is something objective about it"—presumably not because it makes him feel holy, but because he finds it calls him away from his feelings to the objective act of God in Christ. Here are the first rumblings of what is to come—a dissatisfaction with religion as a mere subjective piety, and a desire for the "objective."

On Nov. 27 he looks forward to the future, to postwar reconstruction: "Life in wartime is grim enough, but if we manage to live through it, we shall certainly have something on which to reconstruct international society, both materially and spiritually on Christian principles" (*LP*, p. 75). His *Ethics,* which he had been working on just before his imprisonment, was motivated by the concern for postwar reconstruction, and the new thoughts to which he will come in prison arise out of this same preoccupation. What is that task to be, and how is it to be undertaken?

The next significant remark comes in his letter on the second Sunday in Advent. He speaks of how he is coming to appreciate more and more the Old Testament, which he has been reading much more than the New in the past few months. What is it that attracts him about the Old Testament? He mentions several things: the Jewish awe at the name of God, the necessity of law before grace (a typically Lutheran thought). But the really important thing—in view of future developments—is its *this-worldliness*: "It is only when one loves life and earth so much that without them everything would be gone, that one can believe in the resurrection and a new world" (*LP*, p. 79). Lutherans and pietists, he complains, reach the New Testament, eschatology, and the other world too soon. He is attracted by the healthy down-to-earth realism of the Old Testament, its lack of mawkish piety, "Why is it that in the Old Testament men lie so frequently and on such a grand scale to the glory of God, . . . that they commit murder, trickery, robbery, adultery and even whoredom, . . . that they doubt, blaspheme and curse?" (*LP*, p. 79.) We shall have to keep in mind this appreciation of the Old Testament, for it is, I think, one of the important and generally neglected clues to the new thoughts which are to come.

On the fourth Sunday in Advent he takes this a step further. Redemption, he insists, is not sublimation (which, I suppose, means escapism). It is not redemption *out of* this world but redemption *in* it. He is caught by a line in a Christmas hymn by Paul Gerhardt: *"Ich bringe alles wieder"* (*LP*, p. 87), which expresses, he thinks, the notion of the restoration of all things in Ephesians (*anakephalaiosis*, Eph. 1:10) and Irenaeus' doctrine of recapitulation. Sublimation is, paradoxically, *sarx* (flesh), though it sounds so "spiritual," whereas restoration is a new creation through the Holy Spirit. So, Christianity does not take us out of this world but, having given us an anticipation of the new heaven and the new earth, sends us back into the world to live in it as it really is, and as it provides the ingredients which will be transformed in the new heaven and the new earth.

He makes a very important observation on Feb. 21, 1944, a statement which seems to have been largely overlooked in English-speaking discussion about Bonhoeffer. This is about "resistance and submission" (*Widerstand und Ergebung*), a phrase which provides the title of the German original of these letters. Bonhoeffer's contention is that to be a Christian in the world, you have to have a finesse which will know when to resist and when to submit—an elasticity or flexibility of behavior. "Only so can we stand our ground in each situation as it comes along." Here is an important clue to Bonhoeffer's apparent "cussedness" or perversity. In 1933, when everyone was saying the Church must jump on the Nazi band wagon and identify itself with the new movement and so with the world, Bonhoeffer called for resistance (at a time when even Niemöller was voting for the Party). Later, when everyone had caught on to the idea of resistance, Bonhoeffer turns round and says, the Church is turning in on itself, fighting for its own interests, instead of going out and serving the world. "Resistance and submission" is an important clue to Bonhoeffer's attitude to the world come of age.

On Feb. 23, he mentions for the first time in this series of letters a passage from the Old Testament which impressed him deeply; he had already mentioned it in a letter to his parents a few months earlier (*LP*, p. 50) and it would be quoted again later. The passage is Jer. 45:4-5, "Behold, that which I have built will I break down, and that which I have planted I will pluck up. . . . And seekest thou great things for thyself? Seek them not . . . *but thy life will I give unto thee for a prey.*" These words, spoken by the prophet just before the collapse of Jerusalem, seemed extraordinarily apt to the situation in 1943-44. Men must learn that everything they hold dear is crumbling about them, the traditions of centuries. God promises only one thing: they will escape with their lives to rebuild after the debacle. Bonhoeffer never lived to see the promise fulfilled in his own case. But, as he later indicates when he returns to this passage in "Thoughts on the Baptism of D. W. R." (*LP*, p. 137), a younger generation will live through it and it will be their task to face the loss of everything and to rebuild. Bonhoeffer is here coming to realize that a great deal must go following the war, a great deal to which he was personally very much attached. Not that the coming generation will be without resources. The question is: What must be let go, and what ought to be preserved? Bonhoeffer is open to the prospect of a "reluctant revolution"—of having to say goodbye to much of the extra baggage that has been accumulated over the years, but which is not essential to Christianity, baggage which has become an impediment to the fulfillment of the Christian's task in the new age.

On March 9 Bonhoeffer reports that he has been studying history—the history of the secularist movement in the thirteenth century. It comes out, he says, in Walther, in the *Nibelungen,* and in *Parsifal.* It is quite different from the secularism of the Renaissance, which continued in the Enlightenment. It was not an emancipated secularism, for though anticlerical, it was still Christian. It was characterized by the values of "humanism, humanity, tolerance, tenderness and moderation"—all this over against the clericalism of the papal establishment. Maybe we have here an important clue to Bonhoeffer's impending development: Here, for the first time we find the concept of a secularism which is Christian and yet not "religious," but also not secularist in the sense of the Renaissance or the Enlightenment. It is a lay Christianity. He does not tell us much more about it, but one can see the direction in which his mind is beginning to work.

On March 19 Bonhoeffer complains of finding it difficult to read the Bible—"another spell" he says (*LP*, p. 112), as though he had gone through similar periods before. He is inclined to dismiss it as just a psychological process, and is sure he will soon return to the Bible with renewed zest. It is worth mentioning, because many attempts, as we have already noted, have been made to explain or to explain away Bonhoeffer's latest thinking—of which we are now on the threshold—on psychological grounds; that in the depression occasioned by prison life, the prospects of national collapse, and his own personal fate, Bonhoeffer simply lost his faith. Bonhoeffer was not immune from depression, but as we see from *Life Together,* he knew enough about the devotional life not to take it too seriously: above all, not to deduce anything from it about ultimate reality. He would have agreed with the Psalmist: "And I said, This is my infirmity: but I will remember the years of the right hand of the most High" (Ps. 77:10). All the way through this period we see that this is exactly what he is doing. Witness his constant living through the liturgical traditions of his church, through Passiontide and Easter, the Great Forty Days, the Ascension, and Pentecost. All these, I think, appealed to him objectively rather than subjectively—that is to say, not for the experiences they stimulate in one, but for their representation of the mighty acts of God in Christ.

Much of the foregoing reflections must have provided the matrix in which were molded those thoughts that Bonhoeffer sprang upon the world for the first time in his letter of April 30, 1944. The first part of that great letter is worth examining more closely. First, he is conscious of the tremendous events taking place in the world outside, and the consequences these will have on his life and that of his correspondent. For one thing, Bonhoeffer knew about the plot on Hitler's life, which was soon to come to a head. He also was apparently aware that the allied landings on the European mainland were impending. Coupled as this was with the Russian advances from the East, there could be no doubt that the days of the Third Reich were numbered. Soon, very soon, Christians in Germany would have to face new decisions, and Bonhoeffer is impelled to give shape to his thoughts—this and not depression or loss of faith is the background in which his new thoughts are emerging. Note how he again explicitly mentions Jer. 45:5 in this connection (*LP*, p. 121), and incidentally mentions that he is still reading the Bible every morning and night. The period of dryness has passed! Now we arrive at the moment of discovery. In this same paragraph he launches it:

The thing that keeps coming back to me is, what *is* Christianity, and indeed, who is Christ, for us to-day? The time when men could be told everything by means of words, whether theological or simply pious, is over, and so is the time of inwardness and conscience, which is to say the time of religion as such.

For nine hundred years Christians and non-Christians had a common ground, namely, "religion" (what Bonhoeffer means by that we shall try to put together later; here we are just watching him evolve his thought). This common ground, he believes, is already lost on both sides. Not even Christians (if they are honest with themselves, and not just sentimentally clinging to outmoded associations) really accept it. History suggests that "religion" was just a temporary phase of human evolvement, and that the period of religion is rapidly passing.

What then is the Church to do in this situation? It can do one of two things. Either it can retreat to the ghetto of religion (and thus be dishonest with itself and with the world), and try to persuade a few others to join the ghetto (the one or two who are intellectually dishonest), "to fall upon one or two unhappy people in their weakest moment and force upon them a sort of religious coercion" (*LP*, p. 122), or there must be some other way. During the phase that is now passing, Christianity had assumed the guise of religion (not always the same guise, for its religious form has constantly changed down the years). Now that the religious premise is going, Christianity must assume a new guise. It must become (here comes one of the famous slogans) a "religionless Christianity." At this point Bonhoeffer appeals to the earlier Barth of the *Epistle to the Romans*. Barth had reinterpreted "circumcision" in that Epistle precisely as "religion," thus opposing the gospel to all human religion. Unfortunately, somewhere along the road, a sort of hardening of the arteries had set in, in Barth's theology, and in place of the prophecy of the *Römerbrief* we got the *Church Dogmatics* with their positivism of revelation. Bonhoeffer returns to this charge against Barth in the letter of May 5. Having begun his critique of religion, Barth had set in its place a dogmatism which says in effect, "Take it or leave it: Virgin Birth, Trinity—and if you take it, you must swallow it as a whole" (*LP*, p. 126).

To return to the great letter of April 30: Bonhoeffer proceeds to ask a series of questions about God, Christ, the

Church (church parish, preaching, Christian life). How can we speak of them in a nonreligious way? He is clearer about how we do *not*. God for instance is *not* to be spoken of in *metaphysical* terms (Article I!), or in terms of what he calls "inwardness" (presumably, religious experience). Christ is not an object of religious devotion (presumably, singing hymns to "Jesus, lover of my soul") but the Lord of the world. Church is still there: there is church with a small "c," presumably the parish church and its activities, though there is a hint that these must come under review. There are still preaching, Christian life, worship, prayer, and secret discipline. That, incidentally, disposes of the idea of the Archbishop of Canterbury, in his reply to *Honest to God,* that "religionless Christianity" proposes to scrap these characteristic activities.[3] But these things are, it seems, to be done in a new way. How? There is only one slight hint here, where he speaks of the Church as the *ekklesia,* "those who are called forth. They must not regard themselves as a group of people who are religiously specially favoured, but as a group which belongs wholly to the world" (*LP,* p. 123). Unfortunately, there are no further hints what this might mean. The letter broke off originally at this point, and was to have gone to the post. When he found he could write further, Bonhoeffer pitched in again at a different point—the parallel between religion and Barth's treatment of circumcision in his *Epistle to the Romans.* This leads to a new point. Bonhoeffer has noted, in his contact with his fellow prisoners, warders, etc., that he finds it much easier to talk about God to nonreligious people (note that this is not the Englishman's characteristic shyness about "religion," but springs from something much deeper). The reason is, he finds, that religious people are always inclined to bring God in as a *deus ex machina* to solve insoluble problems, or to rescue them from their failures. As

he wrote a little later in his poem "Christians and Unbe-
lievers":

> Men go to God when they are sore bestead
> Pray to him for succour, for his peace, for bread.
> For mercy for them sick, sinning or dead:
> All men do so, Christian and unbelieving. (*LP*, p. 167.)

It is as if we are trying to make room for God, always on
the fringes of life. This is a third aspect of what Bonhoeffer
means by "religion." Instead, he says:

> I should like to speak of God not on the borders of life, but
> at its centre, not in weakness, but in strength, not therefore in
> man's suffering and death but in his life and prosperity. On the
> borders it seems to me better to leave the problem unsolved. . . .
> God is the "beyond" in the midst of our life (*LP*, p. 124).

It is interesting to find that Bonhoeffer has come to this conclusion through his reading of the Old Testament, for the
Old Testament is full of the God who is the " 'beyond' in
the midst of our life." When we read the New Testament
and its eschatological proclamation we can perhaps more
easily forget it. (Yet what of the Incarnation itself?)

At the end of the letter Bonhoeffer adds that he hopes
soon to be writing more about the shape of religionless
Christianity—the subject he broke off halfway and did not
then return to.

Next time, however (May 5), he does not revert to the subject but instead expresses himself on Bultmann's famous essay on demythologizing (which had been circulated in mime-
ograph in 1941). Paradoxically, as is well known, he accuses
Bultmann not of going too far, as most people in the
churches thought and still think, but of not going far enough.
Bultmann demythologized the mythological conceptions, the

miracles, the ascension, and the like,* but left the Christ event as the act of God and faith itself intact. Instead, demands Bonhoeffer, God and faith must be interpreted "nonreligiously." Here he reminds his correspondent what he means by "interpret in a religious sense": religious interpretation means interpreting in a metaphysical and individualistic way. This repeats the definition in the letter of April 30. But then he adds a remark which explains a little more clearly his gravamen against individualism: he means the individual's preoccupation with the salvation of his own soul. Modern man, whether inside the Church or out of it, is not really concerned about his own personal salvation in the old-fashioned pietistic way. It may sound shocking, but there is no need to worry, because after all it is not really biblical. Certainly it is not Old Testament, and it is not in Rom. 3:14 ff., for the climax of the opening chapters of Romans is that God alone is righteous. Then comes another painfully true observation, which, I suppose, deals with the protest against the metaphysical as the previous point had dealt with the protest against individualism: "It is not with the next world that we [*sc.* contemporary man] are concerned, but with this world as created and preserved and set subject to laws and atoned for and made new" (*LP*, p. 126). Let us ask ourselves: Do we really sing the medieval and Victorian hymns about heaven with any more gusto than we sing "Jesus, lover of my soul"?

We are still waiting for some further sketch of the shape of religionless Christianity, but the whole subject is dropped for several letters. Bonhoeffer does, however, make one im-

---

* This is not quite fair: in his essay Bultmann was concerned precisely with the central affirmations of the Christian message, the death and resurrection of Christ.

portant and relevant point on May 20, though quite incidentally and in another connection. He is speaking of the
love of God (note that there is place for the love of God in
a "religionless" Christianity). This love of God with all our
hearts he calls a *"cantus firmus"* (*LP*, pp. 131 f.), not compromising or diminishing our earthly affections, but providing them with the proper counterpoint. Interestingly, he
calls this a musical reflection of the Chalcedonian formula,
in which both the love of God and earthly affections have
their full reality, neither compromising the other, like the
divine and human natures in Christ, "without confusion and
yet distinct." Perhaps here we have a glimpse of the place of
worship, prayer, and secret discipline, which Bonhoeffer still
spoke of preserving in religionless Christianity in his letter
of April 30. They provide the *cantus firmus* to life in the
world, not an escape from it.

The next block of relevant material occurs in "Thoughts
on the Baptism of D. W. R.," a remarkable document addressed to a grand-nephew, the first of a new generation to be
born and baptized in Bonhoeffer's family. It is full of the
sense that the German people and Church stand on the brink
of a revolution, in which everything the Bonhoeffer and related families have stood for will be overthrown: "By the
time you are grown up, the old country parsonage and the
old town villa will belong to a vanished world." In these
unsettled times, however, the boy will have the shelter of the
traditions of his parents' families. His uncle hopes the child
will not grow up in a ghetto of the past, but will take the
resources of family and tradition and contribute them to
the rebuilding of society. What form that will take, he still
does not see clearly. He knows that the Church in Germany
has made a great mistake during the confessing struggle: it
has fought for self-preservation as though that were an end

in itself. By doing so it has lost any chance of speaking a word of reconciliation to the world. Meanwhile all it can do is to preserve and continue the traditional rites and ceremonies, knowing that they enshrine truths which must be preserved, but which the Church no longer knows how to speak meaningfully to the world as the means of reconciliation, precisely because its image is one of an introverted society concerned with its own self-preservation. Atonement, redemption, regeneration, the Holy Ghost, love of the enemy, cross and resurrection, life in Christ and Christian discipleship—all these things are enshrined in the rite and ceremony, but they have become so "problematic and remote" that the Church hardly dare speak of them (*LP,* p. 140). Here again we feel that the time has not yet come to answer the question about what the "nonreligious interpretation" of all these concepts might be. Meanwhile, all that the Church can do is "to remain silent, confining itself to praying for and doing right by other men" (*LP,* p. 140). Out of these two things—the preservation of the ancient language of the Church in rite and ceremony, and the Church's seeking to serve mankind as best she can—will be born a new form of the Church.

There seems at first sight to be a contradiction here. On the one hand, Bonhoeffer pleads for the preservation of the Christian tradition, fossilized as it were in rite and ceremony, enshrining a precious meaning which will eventually burst forth in new and meaningful forms, yet on the other hand, he accuses the Church of being preoccupied precisely with its own self-preservation. However, this is not really a contradiction but a very important insight. In a revolutionary time, the Church must discriminate. There are basic things —atonement, redemption, and the rest—which must be preserved, even in a fossilized state. But not its own privileges and its "establishment" in the world—that it must let go.

The Church is being driven to rock bottom—to see what really matters in its traditions, and what are just simply human accretions which hamper its mission.

It was the reading of Weizsäcker's book on the world-view of physics which led Bonhoeffer in a letter of May 25 to give greater precision to his earlier remarks (April 30) about God as a *deus ex machina*. Ever since the Renaissance, God has been used as a stop-gap for the incompleteness of human knowledge. Where we cannot explain anything, we call in God, like the insurance companies. But as our knowledge expands, God is being pushed further and further back. As Bonhoeffer had said on April 30, so he repeats now in different language: God must be found not in what we do not know, but in what we do know, not to explain our unsolved problems, but in the solutions of those we have solved.

We must not wait until we are at the end of our tether: [God] must be found at the centre of life: in life, and not only in death; in health and vigour, and not only in suffering; in activity, and not only in sin (*LP*, p. 143).

This is what Bonhoeffer meant when he wrote on April 30 of God as the beyond in the midst of our life. One is tempted to object, with Alasdair MacIntyre,[4] that in that case there is no need to bring God into it at all. Are we not then using the name "God" just because we are clinging to a traditional pious vocabulary, and though we can do without him very well, we still want to go on plastering the name of God over the top of perfectly intelligible reality for old times' sake. "God" does not really mean anything or contribute anything. We are, MacIntyre says, using "religious language to mask an atheistic vacuum." But this is because MacIntyre is unable to understand "God" in anything but a stop-gap sense. "God" is brought in only where there is evident tangible need of him and we can use him. That God, Bonhoeffer suggests, is not the God of the Bible, the God who discloses himself in Christ. For the stop-gap God is a God whom we *can* very well do without—we *can* explain the whole history of Jesus entirely to our own satisfaction without calling in *that* God to explain it. Yet in that history the Christians are confronted with the presence of a very different God—a God who is not the answer to unsolved problems, but is the "God for us." So it is in the center of life, in health and vigor and activity, that the Christian finds the presence and act of God himself, and adores him because he is there—not because he needs him to solve his unsolved problems. Faith is always a paradox: a confrontation with an either/or. You can only decide, not argue about it, that it either is or is not. For the man of faith, it is always, "Here I stand, I can do no other." The Christian affirms his faith in God, not because he needs an X to solve his unsolved problems, but because he has encountered him in Christ as the Reality in, with, under, and behind events and experiences of life.

On June 8 Bonhoeffer returns to this edging of "God" out of human life, and traces it historically. He thinks it began in the thirteenth century (the reader will recall his earlier remarks about that medieval secularism which was anticlerical but not anti-Christian). One by one the areas of unsolved problems were eliminated—science, social and political affairs, ethics—and now in our day, finally, even religion. The inclusion of religion here may surprise us. This seems to imply that religion after all has not been eliminated (as is implied in the phrase "religionless Christianity"), but that *God* has been eliminated from religion. It seems to imply, not that our modern world is "religionless," but that it has plenty of religion, yet in its religion gets along without God. This point does not seem to have been sufficiently noticed in much recent discussion of Bonhoeffer, and I believe it is the cause of frequent failure to see the relevance of what Bonhoeffer is saying. For here, by "religion" Bonhoeffer means that which caters to the solution of man's problems. Bit by bit, God has been edged out of the solution of man's questions, so that finally there are the so-called ultimate questions —death and guilt. Here, until recently, it has seemed that we still need "God" to give the answer. We still keep tame clergymen in the suburbs and like them around the hospital. But even here "God" is proving to be unnecessary. The psychiatrist can deal with guilt, the existentialist with death (in America, perhaps it is more and more the undertaker*). If religion means answering these ultimate problems, then it is not so much that we live in a religionless age, but that we live in an age in which God has been squeezed out of religion. Of course, there are still clergymen and churches. But they are more and more squeezing out God themselves, and substituting, e.g., amateur psychiatry for pastoral theology, efficient business administration for pastoral care, and modern advertising methods for the proclamation of the Word of God. And instead of preaching the gospel they are "marketing a product."

It is in this letter of June 8 that Bonhoeffer first formulates the notion of the *mündige Welt*, the idea that the world has now come of age. This world is the world which can solve its problems without recourse to the stop-gap God. It is to be noted that this concept of the adulthood of the world has a very restricted application. First, it is related strictly and solely to the notion that the world no longer needs a stop-gap God. Bonhoeffer does not mean to imply

* The undertakers of California recently threatened the clergy that they would be squeezed out of the burial business!

that modern man has become "mature," e.g., ethically, culturally, or in any other way. He is not subscribing to a pre-1914 doctrine of progress. Hence, it will not do to dismiss Bonhoeffer's notion of the world come of age as a "silly and unprofitable one," to use R. P. C. Hanson's words.[5] Second, Bonhoeffer introduces the notion in terms of a simile in an attack upon current Christian apologetic, both Catholic and Protestant. That apologetic interprets the edging out of the stop-gap God as the great defection from God, and tries to persuade the world to put him back in, where it can very well get on without him. This, says Bonhoeffer, is *"like* an attempt to put a grown-up man back into adolescence, i.e., to make him dependent on things on which he is not in fact dependent any more, thrusting him back into problems which are not problems any more" (*LP*, p. 147).

Bonhoeffer then undertakes a review of modern Christian apologetic, starting with liberal theology, through Heim, Althaus, Tillich, Barth, the Confessing Church, and Bultmann. Liberal theology had at least the merit of not trying to put the clock back, of recognizing that the world—in Bonhoeffer's restricted sense—had really come of age; but it simply capitulated to the world, and "allowed the world the right of assigning Christ his place in that world" (*LP*, p. 147). This is important, because many of Bonhoeffer's critics have thought that he was doing just the same thing, and thus depriving Christianity of its distinctive message to the world. But all Bonhoeffer is doing is pleading for a recognition— such as he praises the liberals for—of the situation of the world as it is, and not trying to make it otherwise before the gospel can be preached to it. Heim, Althaus, and Tillich, in one way or another, conducted their apologetic by seeking to persuade the world that after all, it really did need the stop-gap God, and thus trying to clear a place for him in the world.

Thus the world's coming of age, in the restricted sense in which Bonhoeffer is speaking of it, namely, its ability to do without the stop-gap God, must be accepted as a fact. Polemics and apologetics must not seek to alter this fact, but speak the gospel into it. And he concludes (*LP*, p. 149) with the hint that when this is done, the world's coming of age will be understood better than the world understands it itself. Here, it may reasonably be asked, has not Bonhoeffer succumbed precisely to that stop-gap conception of God which he has so vehemently criticized? Does he not suggest in these words that there is an unsolved problem, namely, an inadequate self-understanding on the part of the world come of age? Is this not the same thing that Bonhoeffer criticizes in Heim and Bultmann: in Heim, when he presents science with an either/or of accepting or rejecting the gospel, the accepting of which will enable science better to understand itself; in Bultmann, when he offers the gospel as the way to authentic existential self-understanding? To that question I see no answer at the moment, but we must keep it in mind.

On June 27 Bonhoeffer returns to the protest against Christianity understood as a religion of "salvation" in the sense of release from this world. This is contrary to the Old Testament, which affirms a historical redemption: Israel is redeemed out of Egypt in order to serve God on earth. So too, the New Testament gospel is not "salvation *from* cares and need, *from* fears and longing, *from* sin and death into a better world beyond the grave" (*LP*, p. 154, italics added). Rather, the Christian hope of resurrection "sends a man back to his life on earth in a wholly new way" (*LP*, p. 154). Here again, as in the discussion of the *cantus firmus,* Bonhoeffer is not eliminating the gospel, but insisting that it must be related to the world. Here he is developing the concept of "holy worldliness" or "worldly holiness." It is another way of saying that Christ is to be found in the center of life.

In renewing his protest (June 30) against the stop-gap, *deus-ex-machina* type of God, Bonhoeffer repeats his charges against Christian apologetics in face of the world's "maturity" and against the "methodism" of existentialist philosophy and psychotherapy. He then deals with a question raised by his friend, noted first in the last paragraph of the letter of June 8: Did not Jesus use man's distress as the point of his contact with men, and is Bonhoeffer justified in his protest against what he calls "methodism"—seeking men out in their weakness rather than in their strength? His answer on June 30 is that, unlike "methodism," Jesus does not make every man a sinner first, but meets men where they are: Jesus calls them *out of* their sin, not *into* it. But when he meets a man in health, strength, or vigor, he does not first try to persuade him that he is really sick before he starts to work on him.

The long-awaited promise of a nonreligious interpretation of the biblical concepts is apparently on the brink of fulfillment in the letter of July 8. Unfortunately, however, all we get is some further "preliminary observations," which simply renew the protest against the "methodism" of psychotherapy and Christian apologetic, ending with a protest against being preoccupied with "inwardness" in religion. Bonhoeffer points out, quite rightly, that when the Bible speaks of the "heart," it actually means the *whole man* in his relation to God. But alas for his promise! He recalls it at the end, only to say that it is too hot, and he cannot write any more.

On July 16 Bonhoeffer complains that this nonreligious

interpretation is proving to be a far bigger job than he had imagined. Instead, he offers some further ideas (cf. June 8) on the history of the world's coming of age. It will be remembered that he first traced it back to the beginning of the thirteenth century. In one sphere after another the stop-gap God has been edged out of the world. We might tabulate his survey thus:

SPHERE	THINKER	CONCLUSION
Theology	Lord Herbert of Cherbury	Sufficiency of reason
Ethics	Montaigne; Bodin	Moral principles replace revealed law
Politics	Machiavelli	Reasons of state replace moral principles
Philosophy	Descartes	Mechanistic universe
Natural Science	Nicholas of Cusa; Giordano Bruno	Infinity of space
Religion	Feuerbach	Religion as merely wish-fulfillment

In one field after another it became no longer necessary to postulate God as a working hypothesis. To the apologetic devices resorted to in order to escape this situation noted in an earlier letter (June 8), Bonhoeffer now adds yet another— the romantic *"salto mortale* back to the Middle Ages" (*LP*, p. 163). Instead, Christians must face up to it: The world *has* come of age. They must realize that they have to live before God *etsi deus non daretur*, "although there is no God." This is not a paradox. It means that we have to live before the true God, although there is no stop-gap God, no *deus ex machina*. "The God who makes us live in this world without using him as a working hypothesis is the God before whom we are standing" (*LP,* p. 164). The cross is the denial of the stop-gap God; the *deus ex machina,* the working hypothesis. For the God who is present in the cross is precisely *not* the God who is powerful to help in distress (in the way we expect him to) but the God who is powerless. Thus the coming of age of the world is not a thing to be regretted. The coming of age of the world is "the abandonment of a false conception of God, and a clearing of the decks for the God of the Bible" (*LP,* p. 164). This again shows that by coming of age, or maturity, of the world, Bonhoeffer does not mean that it has reached the acme of progress and the pinnacle of perfection. He means only this, that at least the old stop-gap God has gone, and there is a *chance* that now the true God of the Bible may be heard and accepted. He does not use the phrase to mean the unqualified affirmation of the world as it is.

This latter point is taken up and underlined in the very next letter—that of July 18—at the end of which Bonhoeffer adds the remark:

When we speak of God in a non-religious way, we must not gloss over the ungodliness of the world, but explain it in a new light. Now that it has come of age the world is more godless, and [it would perhaps be better to say "yet"] perhaps it is for that very reason nearer to God than ever before (*LP,* p. 167).

But nearer to God only in the sense that the publicans and the sinners were nearer to God than the righteous Pharisees, and the uncircumcised Gentiles were nearer to God than the circumcised Jews.

In the earlier part of this letter of July 18, Bonhoeffer had turned to the ethical question which was exercising him along with the theological question of the nonreligious interpretation of the biblical concepts, namely, the question of how a Christian is to live in a world come of age. It was one of the two questions for the future first raised in the great letter of April 30, when he asked, "In what way are we in a religionless and secular sense Christians, in what way are we the *Ekklesia* . . . not conceiving of ourselves religiously as specially favoured, but as wholly belonging to the world?" (*LP*, p. 123.) That question had been suppressed in favor of the historical question behind the diagnosis of the modern situation, how the world came of age, how the stop-gap God was squeezed out, and by the tentative efforts to reach a nonreligious definition of the biblical concepts in place of the false apologetic of the theologians. Now, at last, Bonhoeffer broaches the ethical question. His starting point is his earlier remarks about the weakness of God in the cross (*LP*, p. 164). To be a Christian is to participate in the suffering of God at the hands of the godless world. It means this rather than cultivating some particular form of asceticism (we remember Bonhoeffer's apology for using the sign of the cross in his daily prayer: this was not a piece of piousness to make him feel holy, but an acknowledgment of the objective fact). Then follow a whole series of illustrations from the New Testament to show that this is what being a Christian means: partaking in the sufferings of God.

Is this a permanently valid statement of the quintessence of the Christian ethic in the godless modern world? Alasdair MacIntyre[6] points out that it was all very well for Bonhoeffer in the Germany of 1944. In his prison what could he do but partake in the suffering of God at the hands of a godless world? He did live the cross, and it led him to his martyrdom. But is it applicable in this never-had-it-so-good postwar world of today? Bonhoeffer's notion of Christian living can, adds MacIntyre, speak only of powerlessness, and not of the handling of power. All that is left is "being for others" without the suffering, and of this Christians have no monopoly. They share it with the secular atheist who is a sensitive, generous liberal. To perpetuate Bonhoeffer's language in the postwar world is to "clothe liberal forms of life with the romantic unreality of a catacombic vocabulary." [7] There is a salutary warning here: participating in the suffering of God must not be made an ascetic cult, for it would become precisely what Bonhoeffer is protesting against in this very letter of July 21:

> One must abandon every attempt to make something of oneself, whether it be a saint, a converted sinner, a churchman (the priestly type so called!), a righteous man or an unrighteous one, a sick man or a healthy one (*LP,* p. 169).

Compare also the protest on July 28 against making the cross, or suffering at any rate, an abstract principle. And this is just what gives rise to an unhealthy asceticism and deprives suffering of its element of contingency upon a divine ordinance (*LP,* p. 173). To this one could add the attempt to make oneself a martyr. The cross must not be sought out, any more than Jesus sought it out but took it in his stride (Luke 13:31-33)* as he fulfilled his prophetic mission. Otherwise it is not the cross. The demand laid upon the Christian is to commit himself wholly to a God who has committed himself wholly to us. The cross will come, *quando et ubi visum est deo*. Nor need we deny that the generous sensitive liberal can "be for others" in a truly biblical way. But where he is so, we must insist that he is so only in response to grace which has encountered him. Where it is otherwise, his being for others is a

---

* See G. Bornkamm, *Jesus of Nazareth* (New York: Harper & Row, 1960), p. 156. The Passion predictions, which are later Church formulations, must not be allowed to obscure this.

subtle, refined being for himself (which of course is equally true of much Christian alleged "being for others"). For the grace of God is of course not restricted to its covenanted channels, though it *may* be found there!

It is a tragedy that Bonhoeffer never lived to write the book he planned. (See "Outline for a Book," *LP,* pp. 178-181.) For here the inchoate thoughts of the letters would doubtless have achieved more finished expression, and his heritage would have been passed on in a less tantalizing form. Chapter I was to deal with the coming of age of humanity, along the lines suggested in the letters, with the decay of "religion," i.e., the need for the stop-gap God, and to give a critique of the Church's response to that situation.

Chapter II was to undertake the restatement of Christian doctrine in "worldly" terms. Transcendence is redefined. It is not a metaphysical doctrine, but God's otherness-than-man in his being totally for us. The Incarnation means that in Jesus there is disclosed the unreserved being of God for us. Faith means participating in this being of God for others, for the nearest Thou to hand. Here at last is at least an adumbration of the "nonreligious" interpretation of the biblical concepts.

Chapter III was to deal with the ethical consequences: the reformation of the life of the Church, so that she is no longer a self-perpetuating establishment, but the community being for others. Practical suggestions for this are made.

Apart from Chapter II and the detailed suggestions of Chapter III, there is little here that we are not already familiar with from the letters. But we notice how the last of the points evolved in the letters, namely, the concept of "being for others," now acquires special prominence here, both in the theology of Chapter II and in the ethics of Chapter III.

The last three "letters to a friend," written during August, add nothing further to the development of our theme. The "Outline for a Book" was Bonhoeffer's last recorded word on the subject.

Summary of Bonhoeffer's Thesis

Let us attempt to summarize the main points of Bonhoeffer's thesis:

1. Man has come of age. This means that he can solve his own problems without "religion."
2. "Religion" means:
    (a) metaphysical doctrines of an abstract kind.
    (b) the introverted cultivation of individual piety, the salvation of one's own soul.
    (c) the use of God as a stop-gap for the limitations of human thought.
3. A "worldly" or "nonreligious" interpretation of Christianity will mean:
    (a) a nonmetaphysical interpretation of God as "being for others" and a corresponding reinterpretation of the biblical concepts.
    (b) a new understanding of the Christian life as a *cantus firmus* of commitment to God as revealed in creation and in Christ, issuing in a life of being for the world, in the world, and thus a participation in the being of God for others.
4. Religionless Christianity does *not* mean the abandonment of the preaching of the Word, the celebration of the sacraments, the inner discipline of prayer, etc. But it will mean a radical reassessment and reorientation of all these characteristic Christian activities, coupled with a ruthless scrapping of much of the accumulated baggage of institu-

tional Christianity, which has more to do with the God of "religion" than with the God of the New Testament.

CONCLUSION

The foregoing examination has been undertaken to place Bonhoeffer's conception of the world come of age in its overall perspective, so as to allow him to elucidate its meaning. We hope we have shown what it does mean and what it does not mean. Now it remains to assess the value and significance —and limitations—of his insights.

Of course the concept of a world come of age is not Bonhoeffer's own. It is to be noted that on March 9—over a month before he wrote the important letter of April 30—he had been studying the secularist movement of the thirteenth century, and comparing it with the Renaissance and the Enlightenment. This seems to be the context in which he formulated the thoughts of April 30. He was taking up an idea of the Renaissance and the Enlightenment, which he found adumbrated in a somewhat different and more positively Christian form in the thirteenth century.

Now it is precisely from the Enlightenment that the idea of a world come of age derives. Eberhard Bethge has cited a passage from Kant which seems almost certainly the source of Bonhoeffer's observation: "Enlightenment is the departure of man from his self-inflicted immaturity. Immaturity is the inability to use one's own reason without the guidance of someone else." * Moreover, as Bonhoeffer is himself aware, he is not the first Christian to learn this from the Enlightenment. The liberals accepted the Enlightenment positively and in-

---

* Eberhard Bethge, in *The Chicago Theological Seminary Register*, Vol. LI, No. 2 (Feb., 1961), p. 32. Hans Schmidt, *Mündige Welt*, Vol. IV, pp. 104 ff., would derive the concept from Hegel.

terpreted man's coming of age, his growth of autonomy, precisely as the work of the Spirit of God. But, as we have seen, Bonhoeffer rejected the liberal solution as a capitulation to the world (see above, p. 150). The conservative theologians have been equally aware of the self-conscious autonomy of the Enlightenment. But their reaction was negative. They dubbed it secularism and regarded it as the *grosser Abfall,* the great defection from God *(LP,* May 30, p. 146).* Because he rejects this conservative reaction, Bonhoeffer has frequently been misunderstood as though he himself had capitulated to the Enlightenment like the liberals. (That, I believe, is why Professor Hanson dismisses the notion of a world come of age as "silly.") But although, unlike the conservatives, Bonhoeffer takes up and uses positively the concept of a "world come of age," he is not, like the liberals, accepting the Enlightenment at its own estimation. The Enlightenment believes that it has established the autonomy of man over against God altogether. Bonhoeffer says, Yes, it has established the autonomy of man from God—not however from the God of the Bible, but only from the God of "religion," the metaphysical, individualistic God, and above all the stop-gap God. To this extent the Enlightenment is perfectly right, and the conservative theologians are wrong. For the conservative theologians are trying to reimpose upon the world come of age the God of religion, not the God of the Bible. Moreover, the organized Church is "kidding itself" into thinking it believes in the God of the Bible, when all it is doing is repristinating the God of religion, which it does not and cannot believe in unless (like most of the clergy and the clericalized laity) it withdraws into a ghetto of "religion,"

* For a recent example of this reaction, cf. Harry Blamires, *The Christian Mind* (London: S.P.C.K., 1963).

of the "spiritual" life, etc., or alternatively, it wrestles under an intolerable schizophrenia of being modern and autonomous on weekdays and "religious" on Sundays.

Of course, there must be a critique of the autonomous world from the perspective of the God of the Bible. Bonhoeffer offers little or nothing here. Therein lies his chief limitation, and the cause of so much misunderstanding—as though Bonhoeffer accepted the world come of age at its own self-evaluation. In rebelling against the God of religion it did not as a consequence accept the God of the Bible. But Bonhoeffer never clearly says so. He never tries to get under the world's skin, to show that everything is not well with it after all in spite of its having come of age, i.e., its legitimate securing of autonomy over against the false God of religion. The nearest he comes to it is in *LP*, p. 149 (see above, p. 151), when he hints that the gospel may help the world to understand itself better than it does by itself, and on July 18 when he says that "we must not gloss over the ungodliness of the world, but expose it in a new light" (*LP*, p. 167). But he never goes further than these vague hints. Partly, he feels that any attempt to do so would be "methodism," sniffing out the weaknesses of the world, whereas he wants to respect its strength. For that reason he does not like the procedure of Heim, who confronts the world with an either/or, which it was open with intellectual honesty to accept, so that, if the world accepted the gospel, it would come to a better understanding of itself; nor does he like the procedure of Tillich, who seeks to show that the secular world still has ultimate concerns, and is therefore really religious, but by making penultimates ultimate is lapsing into idolatry. But it is not only, I think, Bonhoeffer's horror of "methodism" that makes him shrink from trying to get under the world's skin.

It is, rather, that he sees his main message addressed to the Church. The Church has lost its integrity: it cannot speak to the world the authentic gospel, for it has substituted the God of "religion," the metaphysical, individualistic, provincial, stop-gap God, for the God of the Bible, the "worldly" God. And this, not only in its evangelism; this also throughout its whole life (Bonhoeffer is thinking particularly of the self-preservative concentration of the German Church struggle). So the best thing the Church can do for the time being is to remain silent, and brighten its tarnished image by "being for the world" instead of trying to evangelize it. Thus he writes in his "Thoughts on the Baptism of D. W. R." that all the great Christian terms (atonement and so on) have become "so problematic and so remote that we hardly dare any more to speak of them" (*LP*, p. 140). And this is the Church's own fault, for it has "fought for self-preservation as though it were an end in itself, and has thereby lost its chance to speak a word of reconciliation to . . . the world at large" (*LP*, p. 140).

Maybe that silence is still enjoined upon the Church. Dare the Church speak about integration, when it is not integrated itself? Dare it speak about unity of East and West, or of the once imperialist nations and their former colonies, in view of its own disunity? Dare it speak in condemnation of atheist communism when the capitalist West is just as atheistic? Dare it speak about being for the world when it is still so patently for itself? (Pick up any number of the *Church Times* or *The Living Church* and see what subjects provoke the most correspondence!) But some day, presumably, the Church will recover something of its integrity and will have to speak to the world again. When that time comes Bonhoeffer will indeed challenge us to speak of the God of the Bible rather than of the God of religion, whom a mature world has rightly rejected. But he will give us precious little guidance to show us how. Meanwhile, he challenges the Church to realize that it too has "come of age"; it is time for the Church to catch up with itself in its own thinking and life. In other words, the Church must work out for itself the "secular meaning of the gospel."

8

Christ and Man

by William Nicholls

The purpose of this concluding essay is to gather together
the themes of the book, and to suggest that the conflicting
images of man so far discussed can be integrated with the
aid of an image based on Christology. Such a project derives
its inspiration from Karl Barth more than from anyone else.
He has argued with force and originality, in Volume III of
his *Church Dogmatics* and elsewhere, that Christian anthropology must be based on Christology. The first section of the
present essay will therefore examine this contention, and
consider some problems that arise when Christology is chosen
as the starting point for Christian thought. In particular, I
shall suggest that Christology cannot remain as indifferent to
the question of the historical Jesus as Barth apparently supposes. I shall also argue that a useful image of man cannot
be derived from too narrow an interpretation of Christology.
Christology needs to take into account, and incorporate into
itself, images of man derived from secular sources, although
it may be right to reject the rival images of speculative philosophy. If I am right, Christology cannot be the sole source
of Christian thought, but ought to be its controlling and
integrating idea.

In the second and larger section, I turn to some problems
for the solution of which no direct guidance can be found
in the pages of a man like Barth. These are the problems of

the meaning of language, to which philosophers in England and North America have recently drawn the attention of theologians, and which have been raised in the present volume by the essay of D. G. Brown. These are relatively new questions for theology, and it must be confessed that among the few theologians who have realized the importance of such questions, no obvious consensus has emerged as to how they should be answered. In the present historical situation, the strictly logical questions about the meaning of language are bound up with assumptions about the secularity, which in this context means the empirical character, of thought and language, and the propositions of theology have come in for heavy criticism, usually on the ground that they fail to assert anything, although they are couched in the language of assertion. If that turned out to be the case, it would be very difficult to see how statements of a distinctively Christian character could be made about man. As Paul Van Buren notes, in his important book, *The Secular Meaning of the Gospel,* theologians who have sought to establish that language about God asserts something have usually relied upon natural theology. Sharing Van Buren's theological and logical reservations about natural theology, I am unable to use it for this purpose. I shall argue instead that a logical analysis of Christology will show that Christian language about God intends a particular kind of assertion. At the same time, I hope to safeguard the secular character of these contentions by adhering to Bonhoeffer's suggestions for a nonreligious use of the word "God." I thus present a different solution to the problem of understanding the gospel in a secular way from that of Van Buren, though I entirely agree with his statement of the problem.

This analysis suggests that the word "God" has a meaning, and that in the language of faith it is used to refer to someone. I am therefore able to continue to speak of man as set in the presence of God, and intended for relationship with him, though I am not happy with many past statements of this relationship. The third and final section of the essay returns to the discussion of an image of man based on Christ as the revelation of God and man, and calls on ideas drawn from Bonhoeffer, Tillich, and Teilhard de Chardin to aid in understanding it in a secular way. I shall offer some criticisms of the adequacy of the phrase "autonomy before God," originating with Bonhoeffer and now widely current, as a characterization of the Christian life, and end by suggesting that "theonomy," a term borrowed from Tillich but used, I believe, in a sense not identical with his, is a more satisfactory expression of the Christian hope for the life of man in the world.

I

One of the most original and influential contributions of Karl Barth to theology is his insistence on understanding man in the light of Christology. While the idea of Christ as the perfect or "proper" man is not a new one, past Christologies have themselves relied upon anthropologies drawn from secular philosophers, and in consequence the specific contribution of Christology to the understanding of man has been largely confined to the ethical and spiritual spheres. Barth claims to reverse the process, and to begin with an analysis of Christ before turning to the task of understanding man in the light of this analysis. In this way, he claims to be able to speak of real man, while all other accounts of man are confined to phenomena, to working hypotheses of man's self-understanding. These other accounts are by no means excluded from the picture, but they remain provisional, while the understanding furnished by Christology is definitive. For Barth, man is defined as the being to whom God is gracious in Jesus Christ. Thus, man is with God, and Godlessness is an ontological impossibility for him.

Behind these contentions lies Barth's great theme of the revelation given in the Word made flesh. "We remember who and what the man Jesus is. . . . He is the one creaturely being in whose existence we have to do immediately and directly with the being of God also." [1] The traditional Christological formulations of the Church, reinterpreted to bring out more clearly their dynamic character, as testifying to the action of God, from which his being is inseparable, are the basis of what Barth has to say. But these formulations must appear to many contemporary Christians as unduly abstract, and as saying too little about the nature of our existence as we experience it. They offer no *image* of man, to use the term which makes its appearance at intervals throughout this book, but something more closely resembling a diagram or formula. It is consistent with this characteristic of his thought that Barth denies the relevance to theology of the quest of the historical Jesus. He believes, in common with many New Testament scholars, that we cannot know much about the Jesus of history, and that it would benefit us little if we could.[2] Barth's Christology does not derive from a historical reconstruction of what Jesus was like, or how he must have appeared to his contemporaries. It comes, by way of the classical confessions of the Church such as the Chalcedonian formulary, from the apostolic preaching, or kerygma. It is not the Jesus of history, but the proclaimed Christ, who for Barth is the key to true humanity.

A moment's reflection will convince us that the traditional Christologies come from a time well before the origin of our present-day interest in history and historical reconstruction.

They represent an attempt to explain, in the philosophical terminology of Greek metaphysics, the Church's inherited proclamation about Jesus, which, so far as the historian can determine, goes back to the apostolic community and its witness. In their own language, which is neither ours nor that of the New Testament, they tell us that in Jesus God acted unreservedly in a completely human existence, in such a way that his act of grace and reconciliation, and the historical life of this man, must be neither separated nor confused in our minds if they are to be rightly understood.

It may be true, as a number of contemporary theologians have contended, that very few historical facts are needed as a basis for these statements, that it does not matter what manner of man Jesus was, but how God acted in him. If we know that he was born and carried out a ministry in Palestine, proclaiming the Kingdom of God, that he was crucified, and that the apostles proclaimed the resurrection and Lordship of this same man, we know all that we need to know. Perhaps that is all that is absolutely necessary for a Christology of a purely kerygmatic type, but its abstractness can be filled out, so that we obtain a rounded and substantial image, only if we return to the Gospel stories, and try to make real to ourselves this enigmatic and perplexing figure. But if the search for a reliable picture of the historical person is forbidden on theological grounds as an illicit attempt to go behind the apostolic witness, and on historical grounds as doomed to fruitlessness by the inadequacy of the evidence, our case is a poor one.

Certain contemporary presentations of the Christian gospel, more correctly associated with the name of Bultmann than of Barth, appear almost to glory in the meagerness of the historical foundation which, as these scholars suppose, may be discovered for the affirmations of the kerygma. If

Jesus was a not very important or striking first-century rabbi, and like a number of other Messianic pretenders before him and after him, put to death by the Romans for disturbing the peace, how can we connect the kerygma with the man to whom it refers? Granted that faith does not rest upon the conclusions of the historical scholars, and that its primary and immediate object has always been the Christ who is proclaimed by the Church, nothing can stop educated people from asking rational questions about the factual basis of faith. If Jesus was not such as to elicit from his disciples during his lifetime affirmations which in the light of the resurrection-faith become the clauses of a kerygma, would not the Teacher of Righteousness before Jesus, or Bar Kosba after him, have done equally well as a subject for Christology? And if the answer is No, must we not conclude that whether or not he is accessible to our investigation, the historical Jesus was, after all, a unique personality, of compelling interest?

The historian is always right to encourage in himself and his readers a becoming caution or skepticism about any historical reconstruction to which he may be led, and the evidence for the life of Jesus is certainly not such as to permit this rule to be breached. However, such historical skepticism ought not to be made the ground for denial in principle of the relevance of historical investigation to the logic of faith. It will be a central contention of the present essay that Christian faith is inseparable from historical commitments, and that it takes form and shape within a historical community and in historical existence, that is to say, in the world. Christianity differs in this respect from such religions as Buddhism or Hinduism, which either lack a historical founder or are able to separate his teaching from his life as a man. It would not matter very much to Buddhists if

Gautama had never existed, so long as the ideas associated with him were still accessible. Later Buddhist speculation supposes that he existed also on other occasions than in the fifth century before Christ. Presumably, therefore, he is not really thought of as a historical character at all. But if Jesus had never existed, there could be no Christianity as we know it, and if he was not such as to make it meaningful to assert of him that the action of God could be discerned in his life and death by the eye of faith, faith must involve a contradiction of reason.

This means that Christians are committed to the assertion that if their faith is true, no ultimate contradiction can arise between the Christ of faith and the Jesus of history. The kerygma itself is incomplete in that case without some reference to the tradition about the life and teaching and ministry of Jesus, and a Christology that has little interest in such questions will hardly serve as the basis for a satisfying theology. But if we stop there we are on difficult ground. Can faith provide a justification for historical commitments not otherwise justified? If so, faith becomes a working hypothesis in historical investigation, in a manner which is both offensive to the historian's conscience as an investigator of the past, and vulnerable to further developments in scholarship.

To use faith as a hypothesis in historical investigation is no less objectionable than to use God as a hypothesis in science, and that has been rightly condemned by scholars from Laplace to Bonhoeffer, as will be discussed shortly. For although in the discipline of history there are no assured results or breakthroughs such as may to some extent be looked for in the physical sciences, investigation not infrequently does lead to conclusions that sufficiently commend themselves to competent scholars in the field to be regarded as reasonably well established. Some such established conclusions surely exist in the field of the study of the New Testament, and there is good reason to suppose that their number will be increased as time goes on. If so, it is always possible that historical investigation will replace such a hypothesis of faith, either by falsifying it or by rendering it dispensable. On the other hand, faith can never be a substitute for historical investigation, and to use it to fill the gaps in our historical knowledge is to misuse it. If these gaps are large, as some scholars believe, the case is worse, for faith will legitimately be called in question if it asserts the historically improbable.

It follows that the historical study of the origins of Christianity, and in particular of the historical Jesus, is a necessary task for faith, though faith cannot as such discharge it. Whether a sufficiently plausible and comprehensive historical picture of Jesus results from this investigation is not a question of principle but of fact, to be answered by reference to the present state of New Testament studies. Today, most New Testament scholars appear to be more impressed with the difficulty of the task than with the possibilities of providing what faith appears to require. This impression is summed up by Professor D. M. MacKinnon, of Cambridge, in a significant aside in a note dealing with other matters: "It is the fact that the attempt to root theology in Christology (as Barth did) has broken down. . . . What the whole complex of epistemological problems (and that is what they are), raised by exegesis, has thrust on our notice is the sheer precariousness of any image of Christ we may form." [3] MacKinnon is speaking about the doctrine of God; we may hardly suppose he would be less cautious if the doctrine of man were also in question, as it is here. Indeed he goes on to make the same point in connection with ethics.

We need not follow MacKinnon the whole way in his conclusion that the attempt to root theology in Christology, with
which he has himself been associated, has broken down. I
do not understand him to be arguing for the total abandonment of this approach, but for a more sophisticated recognition of the difficulties and complexities, from a philosophical
point of view, which arise from the fact that whether we like
it or not, that is where our foundations lie. But there is a
point of principle here which cannot be ignored. Although
the most recent tendency in New Testament scholarship is
again directed toward the quest of the historical Jesus, and
toward greater optimism about the possibilities of such a
quest, our image of Christ is still "precarious," for what
historical investigation gives, it may also take away. More-
over, the construction of such an image must participate in
the inherent difficulty of all historical investigation. To imagine the past with sufficient success to form an image of a
historical person is a precarious undertaking at all times.
Success is often more apparent than real, and owes much to
self-deception, through which we bridge the gap between
the past and the present by assimilating the former to the
latter.

Whatever details of the life of Jesus historical investigation appeared to authorize us to accept, we should be confronted with the problem of how we are to build up the
data into an image. "Sheerly precarious" or not, our image
will owe much to our understanding of ourselves, and we
cannot hope finally to free ourselves of this subjectivity.
This too is a difficulty which Barth's bold project has to face.
In particular, it must face the fact that we have conceived
Christ, through most of Christian history, in religious and
mythical terms. But we no longer conceive ourselves in those
terms. It is not only the stained-glass-window image of Christ,

the gentle Jesus, meek and mild, of our grandfathers, that presents insuperable difficulties today; even the greatest of the images that we find in the art of the past, such as the Pantokrator of Daphni, or the livid and leprous Crucified of Grünewald, are symbols, however profound and evocative still, of a humanity conceived in religious and moral terms. When Bonhoeffer attempted to sketch a secular image of Christ, he spoke of "the man for others." But even he, it would appear, thus confined Christ to only one of life's many dimensions. It is characteristic of the secularity which Bonhoeffer invoked to be pluralistic, to see life as made up of many aspects and realms, each with its proper autonomy. Love is not necessarily, therefore, the all-inclusive clue to life, though it may rule in the moral sphere. I suspect that the attempt to understand all human activity in terms of love, characteristic of a "new morality" which is being tried out today, while it puts certain moral questions in a more correct perspective, fails to see that other matters must be understood in their own terms, which are not necessarily ethical ones.

Given the mythological garment worn by the Christian tradition in the past, the Christological approach runs the risk of confining the relevance of Christ to the religious sphere, that is to say, of absorbing life into religion and its twin, morality. We increasingly suspect that to do this is also to be false to Christ, but the temptation to do so is increased by some other contemporary developments in theology. For the emphasis on the kerygma has also a liturgical application, and the recovery of liturgy is one of the most prominent features of the life of the Church today. Welcome as this is, it may also become a retreat into the sphere of religion. If Christ is known in the Word and sacraments, which are the heart of the liturgy, we are in danger of concluding that liturgy is the key to life, and that life will become more Christian if we permeate it with liturgy, either by giving all our behavior something of the formal and objective character which is appropriate to liturgical behavior, or by inserting small scraps of liturgy into all the interstices of the daily round. Many Anglicans in particular have felt that this is what they ought to do. But the result is the creation of a very artificial and surely inauthentic type of human existence; and, worse, it is almost certainly to mistake the intentions of Jesus at the Last Supper.

Whatever Jesus meant when he said, "Do this, *as often as you drink it,* in remembrance of me," it is hard to suppose that he meant the remembrance of himself to be confined to a liturgical act. Granted that he may well have intended, as the Church came to understand him to have intended, to provide a means for the regularly repeated renewal of the eschatological act of his Passion and resurrection, surely that act itself is grossly misunderstood if it is supposed merely to have provided a foundation for "the spiritual life," that is, for what I have called the religious and moral sphere. If, in a pluralistic culture like ours, religion and morality, whether coextensive with each other or not, are only departments of life, a Christ confined to these departments is no longer the Lord of the world. Some try to resolve the difficulty by moralizing the whole of life, and making morality the key to understanding life. But the refusal to see the whole of life in moral terms is a healthy one, and even the apparent moral shallowness of *l'homme moyen sensuel* testifies to an insight profounder than that of the moralist, for it reminds us that the life of the senses can affirm the being of what God has actually made, whereas morality only affirms what ought to be, in the eyes of the moralist, and is not yet, perhaps may never be.

Christ can be acknowledged as the Lord of the world today only if his followers learn to liberate themselves from undue preoccupation with a special sector, concentration upon which, to the virtual exclusion of rich areas of creative and constructive life in the sphere of intellect and emotion, can hardly be healthy. Abundant life, which the Fourth Gospel tells us Christ came to bring, is not to be identified with the constrictive and conscience-ridden existence in which so many Christians believe they ought to be at home. Nor is it wholly to be confined to the next world. To confine Christ in ways like these is surely to minister to atheism more effectively than the work of any of the antireligionists of our time. For myself, too, I know that any image of Christ I can find tolerable must show him finding meaning in the world as it is, in man as well as in nature, and not only in the eschatological otherworldliness of his people and times, or perhaps more exactly, of his own (conceivably near-Essene) religious background. I allow myself to believe that the Gospels, if not the theologians, encourage or at least permit me to entertain such a view. Perhaps we have not asked enough of our image of Christ; if we ask solutions to no problems more earthy than those which occur in theological colleges, we may get no more than we have asked for.

An image of Christ which is constructed to meet the preoccupations of religious people is therefore inadequate. How can Christology escape so disastrous a fate? One is almost driven to the conclusion that theologians, who are apt to be drawn from the class of professionally religious people, are the last members of the Church who should be entrusted with the work of Christology. But something so profound in its importance for the Church as Christology is never the product of the specialist alone. If we think what Christology has meant in the past history of the Church, and how its meaning has changed, we may be confident that such changes are not the product of individual theologians, but of cultural developments in the whole Church. Christ's victory has been understood at various times as liberating man from bondage to demonic powers, bringing light and immortality, providing a means of true obedience to the Majesty on high, dealing with the problems of guilt and self-acceptance, and setting man free for service to the world. All of these, especially the last, have their relevance today, though it may be necessary for us to reinterpret them before they can be useful to us. But surely each of them in its time corresponded to what Tillich calls the existential question, as it preoccupied not just theologians but men in general.

The hope for an adequate Christology in our own time does not lie in the wisdom and skill of theologians alone, however well grounded they may be in biblical exegesis or in the history of Christian thought. It lies in the capacity of Christians in general, and indeed of sympathetic observers who would not call themselves Christians, to demand from the richness of the biblical witness an image of Christ which can make sense of being a man today. As we have remarked, the Barthian objection to this procedure is that it must be subjective, even man-centered. In Barth's view, the kerygma is not the answer to man's questions about himself, but itself sets the questions, questions which would not have occurred to man unaided. Only if it does this will it be God's Word to man.

But only man can hear a word addressed to man. How can he hear what the word really is? Barth suggests that a "scientific" exegesis of Scripture, leading to a Christology in harmony with that of the ancient Church, will provide a contemporary form of the kerygma which will retain its objective character as a Word of God to man, coming from outside the human situation. But what Barthians, and to some extent Barth himself, offer as their version of this kerygma is a relatively conservative, and certainly in our sense religious, theological position. Can Barthian theology articulate the Word of God, not merely for our time but for all time? Barth himself would not claim anything of the sort, and he would be the first to admit that theology must be done over again in every epoch. If so, no theology can be completely objective. Since the Word of God does not change, the appearance of fresh theologies must be due to the fact that man continues to ask new questions. God's Word is differently heard when different questions are asked, even if it is not in itself the answer to man's questions.

The questions of today are secular questions, not religious ones, and a contemporary Christology will have to meet them or it will simply not be listened to. It will be useless to reply that God, not man, asks the questions, if the questions we say he is asking are purely religious ones about sins and conversion and evangelism and the like. For we no longer believe that God is a pietist; at least, only a minority of contemporary men can successfully condition themselves to suppose that they do believe this. Is it not worthier of God to suppose that he is interested in the whole of human life, for after all he made it in all its complexity?

It seems to me that we have to conclude that the attempt to derive Christianity from Christology has indeed broken down, as MacKinnon suggests, if we must understand Christology as strictly as Barth does. A doctrine based on the apostolic kerygma and codified in the manner of the ancient Church is still a doctrine, even though it may be further enriched by the dynamic theology of the Reformers and the insights of contemporary exegesis. This doctrine, even leaving aside the inadequacies of any doctrine, to which I have drawn attention above, is itself the result of past and present human preoccupation, and not simply God's unmodified Word. Even Barth's own theology cannot escape subjectivity. But avoidance of subjectivity has been made the ground for cutting theology off from other forms of human thought, and in the sphere of anthropology this means that we dare not make use of what contemporary thought tells us about man's self-understanding. The natural result, in the hands of lesser, and therefore perhaps more consistent, men than Barth is to confine Christology to religion.

What we must do is to admit that Christology itself is the work of men, and therefore of men in their time. We shall necessarily bring to Christology our questions, if not our answers, about man, and hope to find in Christ some sort of illumination for our struggling minds. And so far as contemporary thought does provide provisional answers, and I think that other contributors to this book have made it difficult to suppose that it is entirely devoid of answers, these answers will find their way into our Christology as well as our anthropology. So we need to modify Barth's picture somewhat, without necessarily abandoning it. As Keith R. Bridston has suggested in his essay, Christian anthropology need not set up a rival view of man to the secular ones which prevail today, and must not, at the cost of depriving itself of the truth they contain. Nor must it, as I have myself suggested would be the Barthian type of error, presume that all that Christianity has to say about man can be deduced from a Chalcedonian Christology. The relationship of Christology and anthropology will be more complicated than that. Our Christology must be richer than doctrine alone can provide, for it must integrate a convincing historical picture of Jesus with the high Christology of the kerygma and of Church doctrine, and in thus constructing an image of the humanity of Christ which can serve as the ground for anthropological thought, it will draw upon existing anthropological thought in its very interpretation of Christ.

Our image of man will inevitably suffer the limitations of all human thought. It will have arisen at a particular time and place in history, and may not do as well for the men of other times and places. It can claim no privileged or absolute status, and the attempt to give it such status can only limit it further. The Barthian armor-plate will turn into a prison. How then can our anthropology echo God's Word about man? Only by allowing as honest a picture of Jesus as our historical and theological resources can combine to give us to be the integrating image in all our thought about man. Christology, so understood, can make sense out of our confused image of ourselves, but it must be our images that it takes and remolds so that they do make sense. And the images that it must take today will have to be secular ones, for the religious ones have no life left in them.

II

Here, however, we encounter a new and formidable difficulty, and the more courageously we confront it, the more crucial and far-reaching it appears to be. To conceive Christ, and therefore man, in secular terms is no apologetic option, but an intrinsic necessity of honest understanding of ourselves, even if we are believers. We are all secular men, and we are therefore the men of whom it is being said with increasing certainty that for them God is dead. It is not merely the religious image of Christ that is without remaining life, but even our talk about God. The "eclipse of God," as Martin Buber puts it, is the result not of human rebellion against a celestial tyrant, as perhaps Nietzsche thought; nor, as conservative Christians suppose, of a demonic attempt on man's part to dethrone God. It is the result of the dominance in our culture of a way of thought that we call empirical, which makes it immensely difficult to conceive what the word "God" could mean, let alone whether it refers to anyone.

To say that God is dead is therefore just the most dramatic way of saying (what we have already acknowledged) that contemporary man no longer experiences life in a religious way. If the philosophers whose work seeks to give the clearest possible expression to an empirical mode of thinking are right, what has to be reckoned with is less dramatic indeed, but far more devastating to traditional faith. The very word "God" is meaningless, and it makes no more sense to say that God is dead than it does to use the classical affirmations of faith. Once we become aware of this difficulty we can proceed no further until we have either yielded to it or discerned a pathway through it.

This is the difficulty confronted by Van Buren in *The Secular Meaning of the Gospel.* Recognizing, as contemporary Christians must, that he must seek a secular interpretation of the gospel not in order to solve a "problem of communication," but in order to understand it himself, he turns to linguistic analysis as a suitable philosophical tool. When he does so, however, he finds the difficulty overwhelming, and considers himself forced to concede that speech about God cannot be assigned a cognitive meaning. Whatever meaning may be extracted from it by patient analysis, and Van Buren is confident that there is meaning to be found, such language tells us nothing about what is the case. Van Buren's secular interpretation of the gospel accordingly eliminates talk about God in the sense of a transcendent being, and considers faith as an interpretative insight (or *blik,* in a term borrowed from R. M. Hare) about the world. What results may be termed an atheistic ortho-doxy of no little brilliance.

What drove Van Buren to this radical, even startling, con-clusion? Apparently one of the principal reasons, in his own mind, is his intellectual loyalty to Karl Barth, his former teacher.[4] Van Buren notes that those theologians and Chris-tian philosophers who have been most active, in the dialogue with the logical empiricists, in seeking to give a cognitive meaning to religious propositions have done this through a revived and reworked natural theology. Van Buren, on the other hand, believes that Barth has shown conclusively that natural theology is a dead end. Theology can only be based on Christology, if it is to remain Christian. He is thus, I think, suspicious on theological grounds of the type of in-terpretation of the gospel offered by theologians of this stamp, and this reinforces powerfully a conviction, to which he has been led for purely logical reasons, that statements about God cannot be understood as asserting anything.

It may turn out that the logical difficulties are insuperable, but before we embrace this conclusion, there is an alterna-tive to be considered which is at least *a priori* a possible one, and it is puzzling that Van Buren, as a pupil of Barth's, neglected to consider it, even if he had felt himself compelled to dismiss it in the end. This is the possibility that while the secular meaning of the gospel will be based, as Van Buren himself believes, on Christology, a logical analysis of Chris-tology may lead us to see that the word "God" has a meaning, that statements in which it occurs assert that something is the case, and that the meaning of the word is to be discovered from its use in Christology. If I understand Van Buren cor-rectly, and the passage in which he discusses these matters is not as clear as most in his lucidly written book, he has first dismissed the term "God" on grounds of logical empir-

icism as well as on the basis of the rejection of natural theology, and then turned to a Christology from which God has
been eliminated as the basis for his secular interpretation
of the gospel. But if Christology is as fundamental as Van
Buren, following Barth, believes, the proper procedure
should be to begin with Christology as being in fact the
starting point of the Christian scheme of assertions, and see
where its logical analysis leads.

If this procedure should lead to the conclusion that the
propositions of theology, understood as implications and
components of Christology, succeed in asserting that something is the case when they speak of God, the project will
turn out to have a double advantage. It will be far more
consonant with Van Buren's own proposal to retain the
essential contribution of Barth, while submitting to the
exigencies of dialogue with linguistic philosophy. For Barth,
deprived of what he has to say about God, is not easily
recognizable. And it would, of course, obviate the necessity
of continuing the Christian faith only in an atheist form, a
possibility that I find is attractive to some for the present, but
of whose long-term future I am, I must confess, skeptical.
These are no small advantages, and it will be worth our
while to attempt to realize them. We ought not to assume,
in advance of such an inquiry, that we can find no meaning
for the word "God," although it would be deceiving ourselves greatly if we did not admit at the outset that it is most
frequently used by religious people in ways which, if not
actually meaningless, are easily falsifiable. The task of rescu-
ing the word "God" from its religious misuse cannot be expected to be an easy one, and it is not hard to sympathize
with those who call for a period of silence.

Indeed, I doubt very much if it is possible to save religious
language from the dilemma of vacuousness or untruth, if

by religious we mean what Bonhoeffer means, and what is meant by a number of contributors to the present volume.* As has been pointed out not infrequently,† religious propositions if taken literally are obviously false, or at least explain events in ways which are so far from compelling as to suggest that simpler explanations are much better. But once the believer starts to qualify these assertions, in order to render them less vulnerable to falsification, he has embarked on a process which renders his assertions vacuous in the precise degree that they become invulnerable to falsification. Ultimately, they become irrefutable because they do not say anything. For if nothing can count against a statement, nothing can count for it either, and in that case it makes no difference whether it is true or not. Such a statement cannot be regarded as asserting anything meaningful. Yet such statements are often couched in the form of assertion, so that they may mislead the unwary into supposing that something is actually being said.

Until relatively recently physicists believed that electromagnetic waves required a medium for their propagation, as do waves of pressure found in air or in water. So convinced were they of this necessity that they postulated, as a requirement of their current theory, a medium known as the ether, which was supposed to permeate all space, and to serve as the

* The term "religious" is used in a narrower (and no less pejorative) sense by Bonhoeffer than by the philosophers who have dealt with these matters. Some of the propositions often condemned by such philosophers Bonhoeffer would not call "religious"; I here call such propositions "theological" or "Christological." I follow Bonhoeffer's usage because I agree with it, and think it can shed light on the philosophical issue.

† See, e.g., A. G. N. Flew, "Theology and Falsification" in Flew and MacIntyre (eds.), *New Essays in Philosophical Theology* (London: S.C.M. Press, 1955). Cf. also D. G. Brown's essay in this volume.

means by which such waves were transmitted, whether from one end of the universe to the other, or within the smaller bodies with which we are familiar on earth. The ether was understood to be invisible, intangible, and therefore not directly detectable; but it had to exist, or no light or radio waves could travel from one point to another. The ground for the postulation of the ether was the fact that such waves do travel. However, in more recent years the failure of a number of subtle experiments to confirm the existence of the ether, coupled with a more critical approach to scientific logic, has convinced most scientists that the assertion that there is an ether is without meaning. In consequence, it is now supposed that electromagnetic waves differ from pressure waves in being capable of propagating themselves in space without a medium. It has not been conclusively proved that there is no ether, but the concept has nonetheless been dropped by the majority of physicists. The facts formerly alleged as evidence remain the same, but an unnecessary concept has been eliminated. If in these circumstances, and in the continued absence of experimental confirmation, the postulation of the ether were to be maintained, it could well be argued that it had ceased to mean anything, since the observable facts would apparently be the same whether or not an ether were to exist.

At an earlier date, Newton had introduced the hypothesis of God to account for certain perturbations in the movements of the heavenly bodies for which his gravitational theory was unable to offer a complete explanation. Later, Laplace indirectly offered the classic reply: "We have no need of this hypothesis." Laplace did not intend by this dictum to differ from Newton about the existence of God, but to maintain the duty of scientists to press on beyond all difficulties in seeking for an explanation of all phenomena by scientific methods.

Whatever may be the place for the word "God," it does not belong in a scientific statement. Once the concept of God is introduced into the language of science, it will turn out to behave in the same way as that of the ether seems to behave. It will be impossible to prove that God is not the cause of events in the world, but his activity will be impossible to detect by an empirical test that would satisfy a critical scholar in any field. If the scientist decides to tempt the Lord his God by setting up an experiment to prove his presence, the result will always be negative, and the theologian will be shocked at the logical naïveté of the experiment. It was Bishop E. W. Barnes (albeit in the interests of skepticism) who suggested that high doctrines of the eucharistic Presence should be susceptible of empirical verification. If an experiment were to be performed to determine their truth, it may be confidently asserted that nothing but bread and wine would ever be found. But this would have no relevance to the truth or falsity of the doctrine of the Real Presence, which does not belong in the language of science. If the religious assertion is understood to be scientific in type, experiment will always prove it to be false. If, on the other hand, it is not understood to be refutable by experiment, it will fail to assert anything about the world, and will therefore, considered as a scientific statement, be empty.

The objection to religious statements, as defined in Bonhoeffer's sense, is precisely that they do purport to make statements about the world, and are so understood by those who make them. They attempt to use God as a hypothesis, to plug the gaps in our knowledge. But as science advances, the gaps are plugged by properly scientific, falsifiable, and therefore also verifiable hypotheses. There is no reason to suppose that any area within what we term the world cannot in principle be explained by science, or by some other academic discipline making a similar appeal to evidence. The gaps are diminishing very rapidly, and it is clear that they are already too small to contain God as he has traditionally been understood. If they diminish to the vanishing point, it will become clear that God has been edged out of the world. Bonhoeffer wishes to draw an analogy between this and the Christian belief that God has in fact submitted to being edged out of the world, onto a Cross. Perhaps, therefore, Christians ought not to resist this process, but instead to wonder whether their religious assertions are saying the right things about God.

What I have just said has particular relevance to the doctrine of man. Formerly man was thought to occupy one of these gaps, where no explanation was possible without invoking God. His distinctive existence as a person eluded the explanations of the science of the day. But advances in the behavioral sciences have made it plain, as James M. Gustafson shows in his essay, that we can say a great deal about man without invoking God, and that here too a religious assertion may seem to say something while in reality not asserting anything of significance. Such phenomena as the conscience, "stern daughter of the voice of God," may be satisfactorily explained as due to social conditioning, without any reference to God. All religious experience, so long as it is defined as a psychological event, can in principle be explained, and does not require the hypothesis of God. No human phenomenon necessarily requires God or the soul for its explanation. For scientific purposes, the religious explanation is superfluous, since it supervenes upon an explanation that is already complete, or soon will be, if science goes on at its present rate.

As I understand Van Buren, it was in face of considerations such as these that he determined that a secular interpretation of the gospel could make no use of the word "God." I hope it will already be clear that if God is a religious term appearing in propositions purporting to offer explanations for the world, Van Buren is right. But Bonhoeffer, following some of Barth's most important insights, has suggested to Christians that they abandon the religious use of the term "God" as a hypothesis, consent to live in the world *etsi deus non daretur,* just as though there were no God, and embark upon a drastic reinterpretation, among other things, of their language about God. I am confident that Bonhoeffer supposed that such a nonreligious interpretation of God was possible, and that he was learning to live by one. As a preliminary measure he suggested a revival of the ancient *disciplina arcani,* or deliberate reserve in the communication of sacred truths. He was much impressed, too, by the Jewish unwillingness to name the divine name. There were, he thought, many more times when it was not suitable to speak of God than the religious supposed. To speak of him when one should not was to profane his name, and to take it in vain. To speak of God vacuously must surely be an offense against the Second Commandment. Any contemporary reinterpretation of theological language must therefore guard itself rigorously against falling into the religious trap, and using God's name falsely or vacuously. Total silence is certainly preferable to this.

It will not be surprising, I think, to discover that it is much easier to say what language about God does not, or ought not to, mean than to say what it does mean. Traditional theology has made much use of the negative way, which denies the appropriateness as divine names of the names of anything that we know. The classical tradition of Christian thought about God, which incidentally is far more sophisticated in these respects than even some very widely read contemporary theologians appear to suppose, is so convinced of the utter superiority of God to anything we can conceive that it readily walks the edge of the precipice of vacuousness, sooner than say of God what is false. I doubt if this process can be carried further than the point reached by such a theologian as the Pseudo-Dionysius, when he tells us that God cannot properly be said to exist, for even this is to affirm of him a kind of being appropriate to created things. But this language is so daring that it must seem to most readers to fall over into meaninglessness, and certainly it is more suggestive than precise. Perhaps we may see a connection between this language and what Wittgenstein says of the mystical. This shows itself. But it cannot be spoken of. Perhaps God cannot be spoken of.

In walking along for a while with the exponents of negative theology, I will have incurred the righteous wrath of Barthians, to whom the mystical is taboo, for they suppose that it attempts to form a relationship with, or concept of, God outside his revelation in Christ, thus risking the divine wrath, from which the humanity of Christ shields us. So be it. But I think I may claim that I have avoided another pitfall to which Barthians will wish to draw my attention. In thus pursuing the negative theology over the edge of apparent vacuousness into silence, I have not made any use of natural theology. For all I have done is to make use of an early form of linguistic analysis, more characteristic of the patristic age than of our own, in which the term "God" was logically placed in relation to other terms, and firmly established as in an altogether different category from any other, including that of being.

Some philosophers, of whom Van Buren is critical, suppose that it should be the function of a contemporary natural theology to furnish the subject for statements about God whose predicates come from revelation. If the arguments of natural theology, whether contemporary or traditional, could be shown to assert anything, and also to have logical validity, this might even be the case. In the period in which natural theology flourished, it undoubtedly performed just such a role. By linking the language of theology to other forms of language, it rendered the whole intellectual scheme smooth and harmonious, and enabled the intellectual man to take joy in the vast chain of being that presented itself to his mind, forming an unbroken connection between God and the meanest of his creatures. But this is no longer possible today, if we accept the critical philosophy of the past two hundred years, let alone the contributions of linguistic analysis. Whether or not the patristic and Eastern Orthodox negative theology appears to assert anything, it does not make the traditional Western mistake of trying to derive the subject of theological sentences from an analysis of the world. It takes the term "God," as Anselm does in his so-called Ontological Argument, from revelation, and seeks to analyze what is meant by it.

The negative theology represents the limiting case of such an analysis. It so differentiates language about God from other language that it ceases to say anything that can be understood. Indeed, intellectual understanding is not its real purpose. Rather, it aims to bring a man, as a Zen koan does, to the limit of what can be understood discursively, and beyond it, so that he may be open for the mystical to "show itself," if it will. But the ineffable cannot as such be the subject of language. If we wish to explain theological language, we must turn, as I suggested at the beginning of this section, to Christology. Here too it will be easier to say what Christology does not assert than what it does. We have already discovered that it asserts nothing which might rightly be understood as a hypothesis about the world. The verification principle may help us here. In its present form it may be stated thus: The meaning of a proposition is to be understood from its use; if a proposition is to be understood as asserting anything, we must be able to say what would count for or against the assertion. If theological statements were hypotheses, of a kind comparable to those of science, as theologians have sometimes imprudently suggested in the interests of apologetics,* they would have to be verified by observation of the world. But this point is even more illuminating if we put it the other way round. If theological statements turned out to be such that what counted for or against them was the state of affairs in the world, it would be clear, on the verification principle, that they were really scientific hypotheses. As such, they would have to submit to the rigor of scientific testing, and would turn out, as we have seen, to be false. Christology does not tell us anything about the world of a kind that we might otherwise discover by scientific method.

What counts for or against Christology? The answer to this question will depend in part upon what kind of Christology is being asserted. A purely kerygmatic Christology, such as Barth and Bultmann in their different ways lean toward, would be verified solely by the apostolic witness. It could not be falsified by any statements about the historical Jesus, and in the end it might be vulnerable, as has been suggested by such men as Buri in relation to Bultmann, to the criticism that logically the existence of Jesus is irrelevant

* See, e.g., Alan Richardson, *Christian Apologetics* (London: S.C.M. Press, 1947).

to the truth of the kerygma. I have tried to argue above for a different kind of Christology from this. If Christology is to present an image of Christ that is usable for a contemporary image of man, it must allow itself some commitment about the nature of the Jesus of history. It seems clear to me that a historical disproof of the existence of Jesus would vitiate all Christology, and with it all statements that depend upon it, including all Christian statements about God. Rejection on historical grounds of any particular item in the tradition about Jesus must likewise vitiate any assertion of a Christological type that depends upon it. Christology could be falsified by historical investigation. In fact, of course, the nature of the evidence for the existence of Jesus is such that to the minds of almost all scholars with any competence in the field it appears to resist falsification. The case is otherwise with the particular elements of the tradition. On almost all of these debate is possible between equally critical and judicious scholars, and a rounded Christology will be vulnerable in detail to a negative outcome on particular points of history.

Normally, we expect to find symmetry between verification and falsification. What counts against an assertion, if itself falsified, will count for it. A statement is verified by the successful establishment of something, failure to establish which would falsify it. However, it is clear that while historical falsification involves the total falsification of Christology, historical verification does not go far to verify Christology. If Jesus never died on a cross, the traditional type of Christology, at least, would not arise. But the establishment by historical methods of the high probability that he was put to death by crucifixion does not entail verification of what Christology calls "the Cross," i.e., that Christ died for our sins according to the Scriptures. No doubt, therefore, we shall find that other things could count against Christological assertions besides history. What verifies the soteriological propositions briefly termed "the Cross" is certainly the original apostolic kerygma about Jesus, which involves testimony to the resurrection, however this is to be understood. In other words, the full verification of Christology involves not only history, but also apostolic authority, and is possible only for faith, just as the resurrection appearances of Jesus were themselves afforded only to a special group, for whom they corresponded to the inception of distinctively Christian faith.

Before more fully investigating what is meant by this kind of verification, we may note that this apparent lack of symmetry tells us something more about the logical placement of theological statements. They are not simply statements about history, though they intrinsically involve a historical component. No doubt, a misunderstanding which thought of Christological statements as historical assertions would be less complete than one which regarded them as scientific ones; but it would still be a misunderstanding. Christological assertions make a claim to be true as history, but also as something which is more than historical, and this we have still to identify.

One kind of statement that is clearly found within the Christological complex is the ethical. Jesus gives ethical commands, and Christians take them as authoritative, both because he gives them and, as I shall suggest below, because they seem to have intrinsic force. The New Testament even suggests that a kind of ethical verification of Jesus' teaching is possible. A man who will do the works that are commanded will know for himself whether the teaching is from God (cf. John 7:17). Whatever is meant by this, it is not improbable that other forms of ethical experience, if such a phrase is acceptable, will lead to a similar verification. Anyone who acts upon a sense of genuine ethical obligation might find himself convinced in practice of the rightness of his original ethical insight. However that may be, I suspect that such a verification as the Fourth Gospel implies would do no more for our own purpose than to locate Christology in the sphere of the ethical.

That it is to be so located would presumably be our restatement of the contention of R. B. Braithwaite[5] that the language used by Christians really means that they are asserting an intention to act in a particular ("agapeistic") ethical way, while entertaining certain stories in this connection. Thus, if a Christian says that God is love, he is asserting his own intention to act with love (*agape*) while entertaining stories about Jesus in connection with his sense of obligation to do so. Clearly this is part of the meaning of Christology. It may reasonably be doubted if it is the whole of what is meant. Much the same may be said of the analysis of religious language offered by R. M. Hare,* as the expression of a *blik* or absolute presupposition about the world, preceding all evidence. As I understand him, Hare admits the charge of vacuousness leveled by Flew against religious language, and does not attempt to give it a cognitive meaning. The *blik* therefore in no way corresponds to faith as knowledge, and does not assert anything. Certainly Christology may be a means of expressing one's *blik*, but at least it purports to do more than this.

It is of course a property of Christologies which have come to be regarded as orthodox to assert of Christ that he is the Word of God made flesh. He constitutes revelation, not only about man, but about God, and only about man because his

---

* See his contribution to "Theology and Falsification," in *New Essays in Philosophical Theology*, pp. 99 ff. Van Buren, adopting the term from Hare, perhaps adds something to its content.

revelation is of God. If contemporary Christologies are emerging that do not seek to do this, this is mostly because of the difficulties of religious language. Does Christology permit us to give a meaning to the word "God"? Here two possibilities must be distinguished. Within the universe of discourse arising from Christology, its "language-game," to use Wittgenstein's term, the term "God" certainly has a meaning. So long as we confine ourselves to this language-game, there is no difficulty whatever in showing that the usage of the term is highly specific. The best example that I know to demonstrate this is Barth's own discussion of God's perfections in his great chapter on "The Reality of God" in *Church Dogmatics* II/1. Here a remarkable interlocking cat's-cradle of predicates drawn from biblical, and in intention at least from Christological, usage serves to distinguish God with the utmost precision from anything with which he might be confused.

But thus to locate God within the Christological language-game is by no means the whole of our task, though it is perhaps a neglected part of it. As Norman Malcolm points out in an important article, "this language-game is *played*." [6] Philosophers ought to take seriously the continuing vitality of the community from which this language-game arises, at any rate to the extent of examining the highly precise thinking that takes place within it. Indeed, it might be said that the game is at present being played with notable vigor, in view of the hazards that have recently been introduced. But our real task is to locate the language-game as a whole within the great family of language-games that constitute human speech, and only success in this task will enable us to say whether or not the word "God" has a meaning such that statements of which it is the subject really assert anything. I understand by the logical analysis of Christology precisely this location of our language-game in the community of such games.

So far we have been attempting to do this by a preliminary clearing of the ground. I have argued that the word "God" does not belong in scientific statements nor in statements that are merely historical, though it has a certain place there, inasmuch as it is asserted of God that he entered into a human and historical existence in Christ. Again, I have suggested that the word has a place in ethical statements, but that these also do not exhaust its proper functions. We are left with two important aspects of Christological statements to clarify. The first is their character as expressions of a revelation given in history but not reducible simply to history,* and the second is their claim to refer to a being who is not part of the world. The two are linked, for if God is not part of the world, and cannot be inferred from it, only revelation can authorize statements about him. Conversely, statements verifiable only by a revelation can be understood only if they do not refer to the world. We can reach the immediate conclusion that this language-game is a unique one. We may be able to understand its functioning in part through analogies in other and more familiar games, but in the end there can be no substitute for attempts to speak as clearly as possible in this language, so that its own rules can be discovered and charted.

It will not be surprising if what, for the purposes of one kind of language-game, is regarded as an assertion seems not to be one in another. Or rather, it would be less surprising, if we had other cases in which different language-games incorporated their own characteristic types of assertion. In that case, we could readily go along with the idea that what is vacuous in one game may be meaningful in another. The

---

* It will, I hope, be clear that, following Barth, I understand revelation as taking place in Christ. See also my *Revelation in Christ* (London: S.C.M. Press, 1958).

appearance of vacuousness may simply be the result of logical misplacement of the proposition.

The difficulty which the theologian's, or the believer's, language-game presents is that he obstinately insists that he is making assertions, while normally denying, at any rate under pressure, that these are assertions about the world. But the making of assertions is normally understood as a language-game recognizable precisely by the fact that such statements can be verified by reference to what is the case in the world. Ordinary language contains no category for assertions which cannot be verified in this way. What is involved in insisting that statements about God have a cognitive meaning is the introduction of a new category of assertions, distinguished by a reference outside the world, and by a special kind of verification through revelation in the world. Otherwise, there is no escape from the conclusion commonly reached, that propositions about God fail to comply with the conditions for being assertions.

What should impel us to such logical innovations? If we do not wish to take the language of faith seriously, nothing need do so. Believers who are interested in the philosophical task of clarifying the meaning of what they feel impelled by their faith to say have no option but to introduce such categories of the behavior of language as are necessary to describe the operation in which they are engaged when they speak the language of faith. There is no dogma of logic that forbids the introduction of new categories. The analysis of types of speech not formerly charted may easily involve the postulation and description of a new kind of language-game. Provided the rules for such a game can be discovered and mapped out, and provided that the terms appearing in the language-game and the operations performed with them can be described clearly and without confusion, it can be pinned down logically, and its relation to other such games stated. An example from mathematics may perhaps help to clarify this contention. The square root of minus one is a term for which no numerical value can be given. On the other hand, many mathematical expressions involve its use, and in spite of its lack of similarity to real numbers, sentences incorporating it are not meaningless. Indeed, they are actually required for the mathematical description of things that happen in the world, such as the behavior of alternating current. The term i, root -1, was used for a long time before its meaning was understood. It now appears, to the lay mind at least, to behave in some ways like numbers, and in others like symbols such as $+$ and $-$, which stand for operations performed with numbers. To the contemporary mathematician, i is no longer puzzling.

Statements about God present puzzles which may perhaps be solved in analogous ways. They look like assertions, and those who make them are extremely reluctant to regard them as anything else. But considered as assertions of the type with which logicians are familiar, they fail to qualify, and are liable to be written off as meaningless, unintelligible, or simply vacuous. Once it is understood that they do not refer to the world, and that they are verified by revelation, they can be better understood. It may be claimed that they are not assertions, since they do not conform to the conditions which apply to ordinary assertions. But if they are used in a clear way in a particular kind of speech, we shall have to find a name for them, and since they resemble assertions in claiming that something is the case, and since they have a special kind of verification, for something can indeed count for them and something else against them, they do appear to be a peculiar kind of assertion.

The religious type of believer clings to the conviction that

they are assertions, and so misplaces them as ordinary assertions, with the result that they appear false or vacuous. The
empiricist logician not infrequently takes the opposite course.
He is struck by their dissimilarity to ordinary assertions, and
so insists on describing them in other categories already at
his disposal, or else consigns them to the garbage can prepared for meaningless statements. If logicians have already
mapped out all the categories of speech that there are, and
have found no place in them for statements about God, then
the course adopted by the empiricist is obligatory. But I do
not know what reason we have for assuming this, and I also
cannot help suspecting a treatment of theological propositions carried out by those who appear to believe that the scientific way of knowing is the only one there is. One is driven
to ask if we are not the victims of culturally induced prejudice, leading to the introduction, into what ought to be an
analytical pursuit, of a positive linguistic enactment which
lacks external justification.

Statements about God appear to be metaphysical in the
current sense of the word, and since it has been clearly shown
that metaphysical statements are logically vicious, it is understandable if they arouse misgivings. Metaphysical statements
may be defined as assertions which are incapable of verification, but resist reclassification as something other than assertions. Theological statements look like metaphysical ones,
but differ from them in possessing criteria for verification,
albeit of a peculiar and unparalleled kind. It is open to anyone to say: "I reject your so-called verification. Revelation
cannot verify anything. It is simply a circular argument: you
are alleging that the statements verify themselves, that they
are true because they say they are. Why should I take any
notice of that?" But I think I might be justified in reinter-
preting such a statement as meaning: "I have heard your

kerygma, but I do not believe it. For me, Christ is simply a first-century Jew with some ideas of permanent value." The believer, on the other hand, is saying that he is prepared to take Christ as an authority on the question of God, of a kind that does not otherwise exist in the world. That is part of what is meant by faith.

Theology itself will have the task of clarifying what it means by a person who is not part of the world, or who is transcendent, in the traditional language. That task is far too complex to be properly carried out within the scope of the present essay. Once again, the reader may be referred to Karl Barth's analysis of the perfections of God's freedom, in *Church Dogmatics,* II/1. Barth here rethinks what are called in traditional theology the metaphysical attributes of God in the light of Christology and of the biblical terminology itself and, without rejecting the aid of existing philosophical terminology, finds a richer and more dynamic content for it. What Barth calls God's freedom includes far more than transcendence, but it also deals with what has been understood by this idea. Barth follows Anselm in attaching primary importance to what the latter calls God's aseity. Whether this concept is given in Christology, or imported from later philosophical theology, may well be debated. But wherever it originally comes from, Barth may claim that it can be understood on the model of the human freedom of Jesus, a characteristic which many, including Van Buren, have thought of as especially evident even in such a historical image of him as is accessible to academic scholarship. The rule for understanding the divine freedom will then be the familiar one of removing such limitations from the idea as are inherent in the human level of existence. As Barth understands the idea, even some of the limitations formerly thought to be inherent in the concept of God are removed.

Thus God can be present in the world spatially and temporally, without destroying his own omnipresence and eternity.

A person who is not part of the world is not precluded, according to our understanding of the matter, from entering into the world and into relations with persons within the world. As we have seen, such relations with the world must not be thought of as required for the explanation of events of the world. There is nothing incomplete, within their proper sphere, about the explanations offered by science. If faith says of an event that in it the action of God may be discerned, it does not intend to say that this is an event of which science can give no account, simply intruded into the continuum of ordinary events. So far as we can tell, there is no reason to believe that there are any such events. Whatever happens can in principle, even if not in the present state of our knowledge, be understood scientifically. But faith makes possible another kind of understanding, meaningful to believers, in the light of which events, fully explained at the scientific level of understanding, may also be thought of as the action of God, and thus a means of receiving his gracious promises and commands, and of entering into the obedience of love toward God. Hence God may be encountered in the world, not directly and immediately, but through his action in, with, and under the events of the world.

No law can be formulated to say that God is equally present in all events, or to predict the events in which his presence may be discerned. Such discernment is the task of faith, and of faith alone. Faith cannot be converted into sight by any means whatever. There will never be an event while this world lasts for which an explanation not invoking faith is not possible, and even satisfactory to the reasoning mind. The believer never comes upon an event which allows him to trump the unbeliever's ace, with the cry: "Now explain that, if you can!" Faith can only wait expectantly for the gift of discernment, in the light of which it may welcome the presence and action of God, where others see nothing out of the way. Thus it would hardly be correct to speak of the verification in experience of what has been believed in the act of faith. The verification of faith is only possible in faith, and even what seems to count against faith counts against it only on the presuppositions of faith. Revelation is the ground on which the present action of God is both expected and recognized, and the recognition that the expectation has been fulfilled is still an act of faith in revelation.*

Christology provides the basis for this understanding of God's action in the world. Christology, as a structure of thought, claims to be the interpretation of the normative events in which God disclosed himself to man, so that all other actions of God in the world are to be recognized and understood in the light of his presence and action in Christ. Christology asserts that the life of Jesus, by which we mean a series of events that are in principle fully intelligible as the life of a first-century rabbi, who was put to death by the Romans for disturbing the peace with his Messianic pretensions, is also for faith, though only for faith, understandable as the action of God. "God was in Christ reconciling the world to himself." So faith speaks, but by speaking in this way, it does not annul anything that the historian ought to affirm. In the same way, though not in the same degree, faith may affirm of other events in history, whether in the history of an individual or of the community of the Church or even of nations and of the world at large, that here God is at work, fulfilling the same purposes as he disclosed in the life of

* For the above, compare R. Bultmann, *Jesus Christ and Mythology* (New York: Charles Scribner's Sons, 1958), V, "The Meaning of God as Acting."

Jesus. Human life may thus be lived as a dialogue with God, as opportunity for response to the love disclosed in Christ. If so, the believer will not offer a theory to explain events, whether or not they at present lack scientific explanation, but will decide and act in the light of such discernment as has become possible in the moment.

If such a relation with God is possible for faith, it must be the most important of all man's relationships, in the light of which all others are finally to be evaluated and understood. So far as faith offers a general statement, that statement must be the affirmation that man is intended for this relationship with God, and that in Christ he has been set free from all that prevents him from living in it. In showing, as I have endeavored to do, that the word "God" has an intelligible meaning, and that it makes sense to speak of the action of God in the world, we have done what is necessary to assert a distinctively Christian view of man.

III

We have now reached a point where it seems that if language about God can be rescued from its "religious" interpretation, it can still provide the basis for an anthropology which sees the ultimate meaning of human life as lying in man's relation to God. But we have not got very far in describing what this relationship will be like. In ruling out, with Bonhoeffer, the use of God as a working hypothesis, we have acknowledged the difficulty of giving meaning to much that has in the past been understood as constituting the very substance of man's life before God. The analysis of the language of faith must be carried out step by step, and at most the first steps have been taken in the foregoing analysis. The steps so far taken do not permit us to say whether a clear meaning can be given to other traditional affirmations. More-over, the sensibility of the believer who acknowledges his own secularity has still not been much explored, and we do not know precisely what he will find himself able to affirm. Among the aspects of a traditional religious faith which must be regarded as continuing to be in question is what is commonly termed religious experience, including perhaps the sense of being helped and upheld, at least as other men are not, by God. The idea of petitionary prayer likewise seems difficult to reconcile with the God who is not a hypoth-esis, though thanksgiving has not been ruled out. The idea of providence similarly presents especial difficulty. Above all, as Bonhoeffer himself was anxious to point out, the idea of the Christian as a man singled out from others by the spe-cial favor of God has gone.* Some may regard these as seri-ous limitations, and therefore as objections to our view of God. Such an objector may be reminded that we are not proposing the elimination of still viable parts of the Chris-tian tradition, in order to cut down the gospel to a size that secular man can swallow. Our contention has been a very different one. What I have said stands or falls by the assump-tion that this is a secular age in which any talk about God presents the greatest difficulty, and in which very little that has in the past been taken for granted by religion will not turn out to be without meaning for anyone who is honest about his own secularity. Let us remember that Van Buren was unable to find meaning even for the word "God." If we have managed to find meaning where he could not, and it remains to be seen whether we have in fact succeeded, this is

---

* R. H. Fuller has reminded us, however, of how much Bonhoeffer himself thought should be retained. I would only add a reservation about the interpretation of "Arkandisziplin." Cf. *Widerstand und Ergebung* (Munich, 1959), pp. 180 and esp. 185.

something to be thankful for. We shall be able to succeed in our task only if we are prepared to be rigorous in applying the rules we have discovered.

Thus, to claim that man belongs in the presence of God is now seen to be a very different matter from allotting him a religious dimension of life, into which he can withdraw to encounter God. Especially we do not mean that man is to experience that absolute dependence, which (no doubt at some risk of caricature) has commonly been taken to stand for Schleiermacher's view of the nature of the religious consciousness. On the contrary, secular man must embrace the psychological maturity involved in doing without father-figures, whether earthly or heavenly. It had better be said openly that for many modern men, the most difficult words of Jesus are: "Our Father, who art in heaven." R. H. Fuller has shown, in his essay, how far Bonhoeffer was prepared to go in identifying himself with modern man's rejection of a stop-gap God, to whom we can always turn to get us out of the difficulties we could have avoided for ourselves, or ought to endure as part of the human lot. Indeed, it may be right to suppose that Jesus himself rejected such a *deus ex machina,* if the story of his refusal to invoke him in the temptations in the wilderness gives us any authentic insight into his attitudes. And if Jesus had ever entertained such a conception of God, the cry of dereliction from the Cross shows that he would have had to abandon it at the last.

In an age where God is in eclipse, we can only hope to know him by "unknowing." If secular man is to have a spirituality, an approach to God, it will perhaps turn out, surprisingly, to have more in common with that of the contemplatives and mystics of the past than with the so-called "actives," with their emotionally rich devotional life and practical orientation. For the contemplatives have been willing to renounce religious experience, with all its illusory satisfactions, and go into the darkness, in which God is only to be known in ways of his own choosing, and beyond all that we call experience. But today that darkness is not just the lot of a religious elite of enclosed contemplative monks and friars, but of the ordinary Christian. And where the contemplatives of the past began with a vivid devotional life, and experienced its disappearance as the onset of a painful night of the senses, the present-day secular Christian will probably never have known anything else but the darkness, for the way of devotion will never have opened its gates to him. Perhaps therefore a deeply correct instinct, in spite of very obvious aberrations, lies beneath the contemporary search for a secular mysticism, whether it be in Vedanta, Zen, the psychedelic drugs, or in sexual experience. Nor should the Christian find anything scandalous even in the "instant mysticism" promised by the exponents of LSD, provided only that the supposed ecstasy bears its appropriate fruit in humility and charity. For there is nothing Christian in the notion that union with God is the fruit of hard work, and much in the notion that it is entirely gratuitous.

If man remains, as we have wished to claim, open to life before God, it will therefore be in relatively unfamiliar ways. Since the God of idolatrous religion has disappeared, we hardly know where to look for God. Lacking mystical insight, we have to be content to find him at the appointed place, in Word and sacrament and objective symbol. We shall feel, for the most part, exactly like atheists who nonetheless go to church. Do I say we shall feel like that? This is no program. That is how it actually is, and wishing will not make it otherwise. And how can we have absolute dependence upon a God who does not seem to be there? Must we not, as Bonhoeffer said, live before God as if he did not exist, because that is exactly how we experience our relationship to him?

We are impelled, it seems, in the direction of such a phrase as the convenient summary of Bonhoeffer's view as "autonomy before God." In an earlier essay[7] I expressed my agreement with the contention that the post-Renaissance assertion of human autonomy represents a change in man's self-understanding that is in principle irreversible. Religious people still preach dependence; indeed the difficulties of present-day life have made it in some ways more popular than ever, but its advocacy must fail, if only because even those who preach it do not in fact practice it. When Billy Graham is about to make a jet flight to preach a Crusade, he does not expect the pilot to regulate his take-off time and course by prayer, but by the weather forecast and the radio beam. More seriously, perhaps, when Graham and his associates are considering holding a Crusade in a locality, as I have recently found in my own part of the world, they do go through the procedure of inviting earnest prayer to see if it is the will of the Holy Spirit that a Crusade should indeed take place in that area, but I think he would be a bold member of the local ministerial who would dare to claim that the Spirit did not call for a Crusade in any place in which the Graham team had made it clear that they were thinking of coming.

On a different and wider issue, it is becoming agreed by all religious persuasions, including those who have grave scruples about commonly used methods of birth control, that if we attempt to solve the population problem by dependence on God's will to give us children, we shall soon have standing room only. In other words, the God on whom we thus depend is acknowledged to be an idol, with no real existence. The real God is the one who calls us to act responsibly, with deliberately chosen goals and knowledge of the means to attain them. Where human responsibility cannot be exercised, and this area is constantly narrowing as science enlarges our control over our natural environment, we must recognize that the universe in its very randomness is a moral one, since it does not play favorites, as the religiously conceived one would, by being manipulated in favor of religious men.

The condition of autonomy must apparently be accepted with all its consequences. Among these consequences is rejection of the notion of the boundary beyond which man cannot pass, and where the sphere of God begins. Certainly there may be moral boundaries to human possibilities, but we have a lot of hard thinking ahead of us to determine where they are, in areas where not even a possibility confronted us before. The natural reaction of the religious man to such new possibilities, whether it be birth control, artificial insemination, test-tube babies, or the indefinite prolongation of human life, is to assert that what was impossible is now forbidden by the law of God.

But the reasoning which alleges that these things are forbidden does not always commend itself by its cogency, and only the characteristically religious mind, which I take to be fast disappearing, can appreciate whatever force it does possess. Since we have no way of discovering if an arbitrary divine edict has ruled them off-limits, we are thrown back on the typically autonomous type of moral reasoning, which asks if these things are for the good of human beings. The autonomous moralist may take as his text an utterance of Jesus himself: "The Sabbath was made for man, not man for the Sabbath." Such moral reasoning generally rejects as intrinsically evil whatever is destructive and cruel and antihuman, but of what is positive or pleasurable or simply possible, can only ask whether it is good for man.

Autonomous moral thinking is thus not confined to the new possibilities of today. It is also being applied to things that have been around for a long time, and notably to sex. Much past sexual morality has very properly been prudential. It has rightly sought to protect women and potential children from the consequences of irresponsible sexual union. But such technical discoveries as effective contraceptives and antibiotics are making prudential morality far less necessary. Or perhaps it would be better to say that they are introducing a new form of prudential morality, which says that it is immoral not to take precautions. In these circumstances, many are saying that sexual morality is for human beings, not human beings for sexual morality. Once we separate it from the partially utilitarian function of procreation, and bring that within the sphere of responsible human choice, sex appears in a new light as a means of affirming, with varying mixtures of affection and passion, the created glory of another human being. Once we take that step, we enter a region where the old simple but difficult rules seem of far less use, and only interpersonal terms like affection, fidelity, devotion, responsibility, can afford us any guidance. Part of my point is that these are exactly the terms that a secular moralist must employ.

Deprived of the old certainty of a heteronomous, but from our present point of view arbitrary, divine command, the Christian uses the same type of moral reasoning as anyone else. To find, if indeed that is our task, a special Christian word to say in the moral sphere, becomes difficult to the point of impossibility. The Christological analogy of Ephesians may indeed give Christians a particular insight into the nature of marriage, though there is much in the language of Ephesians that seems to belong to obsolete social customs; but when it comes to sex in general, now that we know how pervasive it is, from the cradle to the grave, we also know how little we in fact know about its right use and enjoyment. And in an age which is looking, as I have suggested, for a secular mysticism, it cannot be forgotten that sex is the only way to a quasi-mystical experience which is open to all adults and most teen-agers, without any need for metaphysical assumptions or a special way of life. To say this is not to give an answer but to ask a question. But I do not now know of any way of answering it that will not employ the type of reasoning I have called autonomous.

Our growing autonomy, which often seems as much thrust upon us as sought, increasingly calls in question the validity of even so classical a notion as the studious avoidance of *hubris*. Many profundities have been discovered, by Christians and others, in this Greek idea, but surely it originally stood for nothing more than the superstitious fear of success. If you succeed too much, something will catch you out and even the score; so watch out, and if you are doing too well, don't let the gods notice. Of course there is such a thing as arrogance, and the arrogance of the powerful and successful is a peculiarly unlovely thing. But what is objectionable about such arrogance lies in the attitude displayed to other human beings, not the success which may provoke or encourage it. We ought not to invoke the dangers of *hubris* to justify failure of nerve. The religious variety of the Christian mind is apt to condemn technological civilization, with all the new possibilities it opens up to individuals and to societies, as unexampled *hubris*. After all, is it not the most common Christian objection to Marxism (leaving aside the crude condemnation of "atheistic communism") that it seeks to bring in the Kingdom of God on earth by human means? But the technological democracy of North America and Western Europe does not differ from Communism in this respect, and presumably therefore does not in respect of atheism either, if the mark of atheism is taken to be the autonomous assertion of what man can do. *Hubris,* in the sense of arrogance, can hardly be avoided simply by refraining from doing what we know we can do. What I have heard called "muck-mysticism," the rejection of technology in favor of an agricultural and rural way of life, is foolish and pusillanimous, and therefore without genuine claim to superior godliness.

There is, however, as Ronald Gregor Smith rightly recognizes in his essay, something vertiginous about the prospect opened up by continued autonomy, and perhaps those of us who were writing about it in the fifties are to be criticized for not taking this sufficiently into account. In proclaiming the end of religion, under the inspiration of Bonhoeffer and others, we were perhaps forgetful of the pain and discomfort involved in the acceptance of maturity, and of the lengths to which human beings will go to avoid it. In the sixties, religion is still around, and there are signs that in some areas of society it is even more flourishing than before. It would also be fair to say that more contemporary Christians are fundamentalists, whether of Catholic or Protestant varieties, than are inclined to a historically critical view of the origins of Christianity or the pursuit of "religionlessness."

Probably, therefore, Bonhoeffer's presumption that the time of religion was already coming to an end should be regarded as an example of what the biblical scholars term "prophetic foreshortening." What is certain to come is seen as coming immediately. If men are to any extent the products of their culture (and Bonhoeffer was sociologically oriented enough to take this very much into account), they cannot fail to be moved toward autonomy and the loss of religiousness. But they may also resist these pressures because they fear them and they may be driven into religion again by other forces, which perhaps Bonhoeffer did not take into account. Mass society, by depriving the individual of many of those meaningful small groups in which he becomes a person by interaction with other persons, also deprives him of the capacity for autonomy. And if Marshall McLuhan is right,[8] the "retribalization" of modern man, through the influence of the electronic mass media, may make autonomy far more difficult for the individual to sustain. If that is the case, we may see the Western world swept by new religious forms, using TV as their medium. The symbolically named Oral Roberts may conceivably be the precursor of the religious leaders of the second oral culture announced by McLuhan.

But there is perhaps a profounder reason why we should have been more critical of the idea of autonomy. Man's self-assertion in an indifferent universe may be a noble or a glorious endeavor, but it can also be pathetic, without becoming tragic. The writers and artists instanced by Nathan A. Scott in the first essay in this volume seem to bear testimony to this possibility. Autonomy carries within it the threat of meaninglessness, since it cannot discover a source of meaning more ultimate than man himself. As has been said, perhaps the trouble with man is that he isn't up to it. And when autonomy collapses, experience seems to show that surrender is complete. In the life of the individual, the youth, living under the tutelage of his parents and growing smoothly toward the autonomy of manhood, is in a far more favorable case than that of the adult who has found autonomy unbearable and fallen into a state of regression in which he insists on having an authority-figure to tell him what to do. In the same way, an autonomous society may collapse into a totalitarianism far more grievous than the feudal relationships which preceded autonomy, as the example of Germany shows.

Is the image of man as autonomous and secular the best that a new Christian anthropology has to offer? I believe that a more adequate image may be found in the idea of theonomy, of which Tillich is, so far as I know, the originator.* Starting from the alternatives of heteronomy and autonomy which presented themselves to the men of the Enlightenment, Tillich suggests that while each testifies to an essential element in man's relation to reality, neither alone is adequate. Presumably the idea first presented itself to him as the Hegelian synthesis of the two opposites. Heteronomy, the thesis, is negated in autonomy, and theonomy appears as the negation of the negation, reaffirming the values of heteronomy in a form incorporating the truth in autonomy. In Tillich's later writings the idea of theonomy has gained in depth and comprehensiveness of meaning, and appears as the root from which the other two have split off into mutual antithesis. Originally he used the term to characterize certain cultures which were open to the unconditional, and which he believed had made their appearance at particular periods in history. I have used it, and use it here, in a slightly different sense, more related to Tillich's own in his *Systematic Theology,* to suggest a way of being human which has not yet characterized any society as such, perhaps not even the Church, but which is certainly part of our image of Christ.

Theonomy seems to suggest a way of living before God which goes beyond autonomy; the latter perhaps still carries with it some sense of striving toward independence, and hence of lack of freedom. If heteronomy suggests that a person or a culture finds its law of being in another, autonomy

---

* See, e.g., *The Protestant Era* (Chicago: University of Chicago Press, 1948), pp. 56 ff., and *Systematic Theology,* Vol. I (Chicago: University of Chicago Press, 1951), pp. 85 ff.: "[Theonomy] means autonomous reason united with its own depth" (*ibid.,* p. 85).

suggests that the law of being is found within oneself, that it is self-chosen. Thus the autonomous man is free even when he obeys the law, for he has recognized for himself the claims of the law, and assents to it from within himself and on his own responsibility. Even autonomy does not mean limitless freedom, but rather the acceptance of responsibility before one's own conscience, just as heteronomy does not mean simple subordination to an alien rule, but the recognition of the objective claims of external reality and of history, at least as Tillich now interprets it.

Our culture since the time of the Enlightenment has increasingly been characterized by autonomy, as I have recognized above. There is no way back behind autonomy to renewed heteronomy; there is only regression to something worse. But perhaps there is a way forward from the contradictions of autonomy, which seems to permit man to come of age only at the cost of an "eclipse of God" so complete that man finds himself menaced by meaninglessness and despair. If, as I have suggested above, secular man can still attach meaning to the idea of God, albeit in a form that conclusively rejects heteronomy, perhaps the idea of theonomy may give us a language in which to conceive his relationship to God. In a theonomous relationship, God does not appear as the alien or outsider, imposing an arbitrary limitation upon man's maturity. Nor is he identical with man, so as to offer nothing which can judge or redeem him. Rather he is found to disclose himself as one who is not alien to man, who is on his side, who validates as he judges the profoundest hopes of man for his life. In a theonomous relationship, the will of God is not an arbitrary edict, but something to which man can give assent with all his being, for it is the fulfillment of what man is made for. The theonomous man finds in love and creative work both the deepest longing of his own heart, and the will and gift of God.

To speak of such coincidence between man's being and God's self-disclosure is for Christians to speak of Christ. Tillich does not, so far as I have been able to discover, relate the idea of theonomy directly to his Christology, as he does to his doctrine of God and of the Church. But the step would be an easy one for him to take, since he identifies Christ with the New Being, and it is one which seems to me to be required. Only in Christ, it seems to me, does God disclose himself in such a way that we could speak of theonomy. If that is so, theonomy will be a gift conferred upon man in Christ, and it is to be looked for wherever men, living by faith in Christ, accept the maturity which God is conferring upon them in our time. It is to be looked for, but it is not to be taken for granted. It is an ultimate, or eschatological, way of being human.

Bonhoeffer makes an important distinction between the ultimate and the penultimate. For him, the ultimate is justification by grace alone, and it appears only in certain situations, which cannot be commanded by man. For the most part, men must live in the penultimate, in a sort of Old Testament stage, where this world rather than the next is affirmed, and law is necessary as well as freedom. For the man of today, autonomy will be the penultimate and therefore normal condition. Theonomy will be the ultimate, which will descend upon man as and when God wills. It is to be expected in hope, but it does not come at man's behest. It may even be prepared for by wise and right living, but wise and right living are not themselves theonomy. Theonomy is not a possession, which could permanently characterize an individual or community. But it remains the object of expectancy and hope, never to be excluded in the

Church, since she is the new humanity founded on Christ.*

Perhaps, indeed, theonomy, so defined, is to be preferred to "autonomy before God" as a description of what Bonhoeffer himself was feeling after. For when Bonhoeffer says that we must live before God as those who can get on very well without him, that we must live and decide *etsi deus non daretur*, it is surely the paradoxical *before God* which is determinative, and which distinguishes Bonhoeffer's conception of the life of the religionless Christian from mere autonomy.[9] Theonomy is the relationship of adult man to a gracious God. Even in the pages of Karl Barth, so often thought of as the apostle of heteronomy, we can find much that seems to correspond with the idea of theonomy. For Barth insists that while God does not wish man to be deprived of the grace of relationship with himself, he wishes to allow man time and space for his own existence as another alongside God himself.† Believing secularity, or theonomy, is a possibility for man that arises directly out of the nature of the God disclosed in Jesus Christ. That God permits secularity is a necessary deduction from the fact that it exists. That he encourages it may be a possible deduction from a revelation in the form of the Servant. The God who stands off from the man he has created, who veils himself even, and especially, where he is most clearly revealed, who permits himself, as Bonhoeffer says, to be edged out of the world onto a Cross, is also the God who endows man with the spiritual resources that have brought about our scientific and secular culture. Thus our repudiation, as secular men, of the use of

---

* For Bonhoeffer's views on the ultimate and the penultimate, see *Ethics*, trans. N. H. Smith (London: S.C.M. Press, 1955), pp. 79 ff., and *Letters and Papers from Prison* (London: Collins, 1960; Fontana edition), pp. 50, 56 f., 92.

† See Barth's treatment of the patience and wisdom of God in *Church Dogmatics* II/1 (Edinburgh: T. & T. Clark, 1957), pp. 406 ff.

God as a working hypothesis, our incredulity directed toward the God of the gaps, which are themselves the product of a culture based upon scientific method, are most consonant with the God revealed in Christ, and inimical only to the God of religion, who we insist shall be all-powerful, but in fact turns out to be too weak for our needs. God's omnipotence is nowhere so clearly disclosed as in his gift of freedom on so lavish a scale.

Theonomy is thus hardly the Hegelian synthesis, but rather the Christological reconciliation, of the alternatives of heteronomy and autonomy. Between man deprived of manhood, and man deprived of God, there can be no real choice. As theonomy overcomes heteronomy, it gives man the right to a responsible and adult life, the right to a proper secularity, before God. As it overcomes autonomy, it gives even to secular man the right to live before God, without abandoning what is true in his secularity. It confers upon man true freedom, which is a reflection of and a response to the freedom of God to be with man in Christ. It calls man to be nothing less than a fellow worker with God in the cosmic purposes which are his.

In the last phrase we have perhaps moved on to the territory which Teilhard de Chardin has made his own. If indeed we are to look for an example of theonomous thinking, it will be hard to find a better one than Teilhard. There is much that can and even must be questioned in Teilhard's thought. And it is perhaps surprising to find the Catholic scientist and mystic appearing here in the company of Protestant theologians, with whom he displays no particular acquaintance. But we may remember that he anticipated Bonhoeffer in speaking about the coming of age of man,*

---

* See, e.g., *The Future of Man* (London: Collins, 1964), pp. 18 f. This material is from an essay, "A Note on Progress," written in 1920.

and he has shown himself even better able to communicate with secular men than anyone we have here discussed. Teilhard exhibited in a striking way the union in one mind of the secular, scientific spirit of free and fearless inquiry, and the spirit of Christian, even mystical, devotion to God. Even his conception of God, questionable as it is in many ways, is careful to avoid the false alternatives of an arbitrarily interfering creator who cannot let his work alone, and of a deist absentee Landlord, who confers autonomy at the price of no longer existing meaningfully. Teilhard's God is radically committed to a cosmic evolution of which man united in Christ is to be the crown. Yet he who is the Omega-point is also the Alpha, and is intimately present at every stage of the evolutionary drama. If he reveals himself in Christ, there is a sense in which he also permits himself, in certain aspects, to be discovered by science.

Teilhard suggests a way to God for secular man, which does not deny his secularity but leads forward from it and indeed arises just when secularity is pressed most ruthlessly to its inherent conclusions. He also suggests possibilities of overcoming another contemporary antithesis, that between theology and science. Where academic theology has attempted to break down the antithesis from the side of theology, by dispensing with the hypothesis of God even in the study of religion, with astonishingly fruitful results in the field of the Bible, Teilhard begins to break it down from the side of science, by venturing on beyond the normal subject matter of science to matters where perhaps it might be possible to invoke God as a hypothesis after all. Much further study and debate will be needed before it can be seen whether Teilhard has thus fundamentally violated the canons of science, and entered, as his critics have forcefully suggested, a realm of meaningless rhetoric, or whether he has glimpsed a way out of the whole cultural impasse. But his vision, as Pieter de Jong's chapter title has suggested, is certainly one of hope.

But there is a better example than any that the life of the Church can afford. No one but Christ himself has fully demonstrated the theonomous life.* What for us is hope is for him fact. Though Jesus lived in a largely heteronomous culture, he did not himself exhibit the characteristics of heteronomy. Yet it would be patently absurd to characterize him as a Renaissance man born out of due time. Jesus' unique freedom and authority do not come from technological humanism but from the intimacy of his being with God. In his own life, and in that which he commended to his disciples, he did not operate by the book, even if that book were the Old Testament, but from the ever fresh fount of openness to God, to men and to the world. His meat and drink was to do his Father's will. As his teaching shows, he understood that will most comprehensively as undistinguishing love. He did not need to be told that love was divinely commanded, he chose it for himself as what he most wanted. Theonomy may stand for what we are certain we see in him, however precarious our historical image of him may be, an inner and inevitable identity between his own deepest purpose and what he conceived to be the purpose and activity of the Father. The will of God did not come to him as something alien, but as utterly assented to because it validated and affirmed what he himself most urgently sought. Even death and the fear of death could not shake this intimate union of aim and purpose.

* So far as these fragmentary suggestions amount to the sketch of a Christology, I recognize that they too must submit to the test, called for above in respect to all Christologies, of historical verification. As they stand, with their somewhat Johannine flavor, they raise historical questions which it would be altogether beyond the scope of the present essay to attempt to resolve.

A Christian image of man will exhibit man as called to theonomy. The freedom and certainty of theonomy are the gift of Christ. Theonomy is secular, and its holiness is this-worldly. It takes the words of Jesus to refer to life, and not to some illusory realm called spiritual life. It is a possibility not for religious man, but for man who has accepted the loss of religion and let it go, who has plumbed the depths of atheism rather than assent to idolatry, but who still rejoices in the daily gift of life as a man.

Notes

1. Scott: The Christian Understanding of Man

1. William Barrett, *Irrational Man: A Study in Existential Philosophy* (Garden City, N. Y.: Doubleday and Co., 1958), p. 54.

2. *Ibid.,* p. 57.

3. Paul Tillich, "The World Situation," in *The Christian Answer,* ed. by Henry P. Van Dusen (New York: Charles Scribner's Sons, 1945), p. 4.

4. *Ibid.,* p. 5.

5. See Paul Van Buren, *The Secular Meaning of the Gospel* (New York: The Macmillan Co., 1963).

6. Hans Urs von Balthasar, *Science, Religion, and Christianity,* trans. by Hilda Graef (Westminster, Md.: The Newman Press, 1958), p. 49.

7. Augustine, "A Treatise on Nature and Grace," *Anti-Pelagian Works* (Chap. 38), in *Nicene and Post-Nicene Fathers of the Christian Church,* ed. by Philip Schaff (New York: Christian Literature Co., 1887), Vol. I, p. 134.

8. Nathan A. Scott, Jr., *Reinhold Niebuhr* (Minneapolis, Minn.: University of Minnesota Press, 1963), p. 22.

9. Karl Barth, *Church Dogmatics,* III/2 (Edinburgh: T. & T. Clark, 1960), p. 203.

10. *Ibid.,* p. 208.

11. Gabriel Marcel, *The Mystery of Being* (Chicago, Ill.: Henry Regnery Co., 1950), Vol. II, p. 33.

12. Blaise Pascal, "Pensées Diverses," Fragment LVIII, in *Pensées, Fragments et Lettres de Blaise Pascal,* ed. by M. Prosper Faugère (Paris: Andrieux, 1844), Vol. I, pp. 197-198.

13. Reinhold Niebuhr, *The Nature and Destiny of Man* (New York: Charles Scribner's Sons, 1941), Vol. I, pp. 16-17.

14. P. T. Forsyth, *The Taste of Death and the Life of Grace* (London: James Clarke & Co., 1901), p. 84.

15. Søren Kierkegaard, *The Concept of Dread* (Princeton, N. J.: Princeton University Press, 1944), Chap. 1.

16. John S. Whale, *Christian Doctrine* (New York: The Macmillan Co., 1941), p. 46.

17. *Ibid.,* pp. 49-50.

18. *Ibid.,* p. 50.

19. Karl Jaspers, *Tragedy Is Not Enough,* trans. by H. A. T. Reiche *et al.* (Boston: Beacon Press, 1952), pp. 36-40.

20. H. R. MacKintosh, *The Christian Experience of Forgiveness* (New York: Harper & Row, 1927), p. 200.

21. Ignazio Silone, *And He Hid Himself,* trans. by Darina Tranquilli (New York: Harper & Row, 1946), p. vi.

22. See Dietrich Bonhoeffer, "Outline for a Book," in *Letters and Papers from Prison,* ed. by Eberhard Bethge, trans. by Reginald H. Fuller (London: S. C. M. Press, 1953).

23. Nathan A. Scott, Jr., "Faith and Art in a World Awry," *Motive,* Vol. XXII, No. 2 (Nov., 1961), p. 26.

24. Martin Jarrett-Kerr, C. R., *The Atonement in Our Time* (New York: Morehouse-Gorham Co., 1953), p. 128.

25. James A. Pike and W. Norman Pittenger, *The Faith of the Church* (New York: Seabury Press, 1951), p. 77.

26. Paul Tillich, *The Shaking of the Foundations* (New York: Charles Scribner's Sons, 1948), p. 162.

27. Rudolf Bultmann, *Essays* (New York: The Macmillan Co., 1955), p. 180.

28. *Ibid.*

29. *Ibid.,* Chaps. 3, 9.

30. Stephen F. Bayne, "The Eucharist and the Church," in *The Eucharist and Liturgical Renewal,* ed. by Massey H. Shepherd, Jr. (New York: Oxford University Press, 1960), p. 15.

31. Alfred R. Shands, *The Liturgical Movement and the Local Church* (London: S. C. M. Press, 1959), p. 44.

32. Dom Gregory Dix, *The Shape of the Liturgy* (Westminster, Md.: Dacre Press, 1945), pp. xviii-xix.

33. See Dietrich Bonhoeffer, *The Cost of Discipleship* (London: S. C. M. Press, 1959).

34. See C. S. Lewis, *The Weight of Glory* (New York: The Macmillan Co., 1949), Chap. 1.

35. Dom Gregory Dix, *op. cit.,* p. xix.

36. Charles Péguy, *Clio,* cited in Daniel Halévy, *Péguy and Les Cahiers de la Quinzaine* (New York: Longmans, Green and Co., 1947), p. 184.

37. Dietrich Bonhoeffer, *Ethics,* trans. by N. H. Smith (New York: The Macmillan Co., 1955), pp. 194-205.

38. *Ibid.,* pp. 68-69.

39. Alec R. Vidler, *Essays in Liberality* (London: S. C. M. Press, 1957), p. 105.

40. *Ibid.,* p. 106.

41. *Ibid.*

42. *Ibid.,* p. 107.

2. Smith: Post-Renaissance Man

1. Dietrich Bonhoeffer, *Letters and Papers from Prison* (London: S. C. M. Press, 1953), p. 173.

2. Max Scheler, *Die Stellung der Menschen im Kosmos,* quoted in Ernst Cassirer, *An Essay on Man* (New Haven, Conn.: Yale University Press, 1944), p. 22.

3. See K. H. Miskotte, *Wenn die Götter schweigen* (Munich: C. Kaiser, 1963), p. 30.

4. A phrase used by J. G. Hamann in a letter to Herder, June 3, 1781.

5. See Samuel Beckett, *Waiting for Godot.*

6. T. S. Eliot, "East Coker."

7. Bonhoeffer, *op. cit.,* p. 145.

8. See Ronald Gregor Smith, *The New Man* (New York: Harper & Row, 1956), Chap. 2, and "A Theological Perspective of the Secular," *The Christian Scholar,* Vol. XLIII, No. 1.

9. See Martin Stallman, *Was ist Säkularisierung?* (Tübingen: J. C. B. Mohr, 1960), for a historical survey of the word "secularism." Apparently Ernst Troeltsch first used the word in its full modern connotation.

10. Wilhelm Dilthey, *Einleitung in die Geisteswissenschaften* (Leipzig: B. G. Teubner, 1914), pp. 356-357.

11. Cf. especially Gabriel Vahanian, *The Death of God* (New York: Braziller, 1962), pp. 60 ff.; Friedrich Gogarten, *Verhängnis und Hoffnung der Neuzeit* (Stuttgart: A. Vorwerk, 1958), pp. 129 ff.; and Rudolf Bultmann, "Der Gottesgedanke und der moderne Mensch," *Zeitschrift für Theologie und Kirche* (Dec., 1963), p. 338.

12. Cf. the study of Pico della Mirandola by Ivan Pusino in *Zeitschrift für Kirchengeschichte*, Vol. XLIV (1925), pp. 504 ff. There is a growing interest, especially among American scholars, in Pico, but a full assessment is still to come. Cf. also P. O. Kristeller, in *The Renaissance Philosophy of Man* (Chicago: University of Chicago Press, 1948).

13. Miskotte, *op. cit.*, p. 23.

14. Paul Tillich, *The Shaking of the Foundations* (New York: Charles Scribner's Sons, 1948), pp. 99-103.

15. T. S. Eliot, *op. cit.*

16. Cf. L. Ziegler, *Magna Charta,* quoted in Miskotte, *op. cit.*, p. 12.

3. Gustafson: Man—In Light of Social Science and Christian Faith

1. Paperback editions are available of: Erik Erikson, *Young Man Luther* (New York: W. W. Norton, 1962); and Ernest Jones, *Hamlet and Oedipus* (Garden City, N. Y.: Doubleday Anchor Books, 1954).

2. G. H. Mead, *Mind, Self, and Society* (Chicago: University of Chicago Press, 1934). See also Mead's synoptic essay, "The Genesis of the Self and Social Control," in *The Philosophy of the Present* (La Salle, Ill.: Open Court Publishing Co., 1932).

3. Ralph Linton, *Cultural Background of Personality* (New York: Appleton-Century, 1945), p. 139.

4. Gerhard Lenski, *The Religious Factor* (Garden City, N. Y.: Doubleday and Co., 1961), p. 93.

5. Bronislaw Malinowski, *A Scientific Theory of Culture*

(Chapel Hill, N. C.: University of North Carolina Press, 1944), especially Chap. 10; see also Malinowski, *Magic, Science and Religion* (Garden City, N. Y.: Doubleday Anchor Books, 1954).

6. See Emile Durkheim, *The Elementary Forms of Religious Life* (Glencoe, Ill.: The Free Press, 1947).

7. Guy Swanson, *The Birth of the Gods* (Ann Arbor, Mich.: University of Michigan Press, 1960).

8. Robert Dahl and Charles Lindblom, *Politics, Economics, and Welfare* (New York: Harper & Row, 1953), p. 28.

9. Robert Merton, *Social Theory and Social Structure* (Glencoe, Ill.: The Free Press, 1949), pp. 221-222.

10. Max Millikan, "Inquiry and Policy," in *The Human Meaning of the Social Sciences,* ed. by Daniel Lerner (New York: Meridian Books, 1959), p. 167.

4. Bridston: A Christian Critique of Secular Anthropologies

1. Herbert Butterfield, *Christianity and History* (London: Fontana, 1957), p. 173.

2. John Baillie, *Natural Science and the Spiritual Life* (London: Oxford University Press, 1951), p. 22.

3. J. H. Randall, *The Making of the Modern Mind* (Boston: Houghton Mifflin, rev. ed., 1940), p. 227.

4. Charles Darwin, *The Variations of Animals and Plants under Domestication* (New York: D. Appleton & Co., 1896), pp. 425-426.

5. P. W. Bridgman, quoted in James B. Conant, *Modern Science and Modern Man* (New York: Columbia University Press, 1952), pp. 86-87.

6. C. F. von Weizsäcker, *The History of Nature* (Chicago: University of Chicago Press, 1949), p. 190.

7. Joseph Wood Krutch, *The Measure of Man* (New York: Grosset Universal Library, 1956), p. 36.

8. Reinhold Niebuhr, *The Nature and Destiny of Man* (London: Nisbet, 1941), Vol. I, p. 97.

9. J. R. Bruner, in *Freud and the 20th Century*, ed. by Benjamin Nelson (New York: Meridian Books, 1957), p. 279.

10. Erik H. Erikson, in *Freud and the 20th Century*, ed. by Benjamin Nelson, p. 91.

11. Alfred Kazin, in *Freud and the 20th Century*, ed. by Benjamin Nelson, p. 15.

12. Ernst Cassirer, *An Essay on Man* (New Haven, Conn.: Yale University Press, 1944), pp. 39-40.

13. Max Scheler, *Die Stellung des Menschen im Kosmos* (Darmstadt: Reichl, 1928), pp. 13 f.

14. Julian Huxley, *Man in the Modern World* (New York: Mentor Books, 1948), p. 27.

5. Brown: The Secular Challenge to the Christian View

1. Sigmund Freud, *The Future of an Illusion,* in *The Standard Edition of the Complete Psychological Works of Sigmund Freud,* ed. by J. Strachey (New York: The Macmillan Co., 1953), Vol. XXI, p. 29.

6. De Jong: Teilhard's Vision of Hope

1. Pierre Teilhard de Chardin, *Letters from a Traveller* (New York: Harper & Row, 1962), p. 127.

2. Cf. Pierre Teilhard de Chardin, *The Divine Milieu* (New York: Harper & Row, 1960), pp. 20 ff.

3. *Ibid.,* p. 82.

4. *Ibid.,* p. 50.

5. *Ibid.,* p. 107.

6. *Ibid.,* p. 111.

7. On his crisis during 1901, see Claude Cuénot, *Pierre Teilhard de Chardin: Les Grandes Etapes de son Evolution* (Paris: Plon, 1950), pp. 19, 20.

8. *Ibid.,* p. 20.

9. *The Divine Milieu,* p. 39.

10. Cf. Dietrich Bonhoeffer, *Letters and Papers from Prison* (London: S. C. M. Press, 1953), pp. 142, 143.

11. *The Divine Milieu*, p. 66.

12. Gilbert Ryle, *The Concept of Mind* (New York: Barnes and Noble, 1949), p. 11.

13. In *Le Coeur de là Matière*, quoted by P. Smulders, S.J., *Het Visioen van Teilhard de Chardin* (Brugge, Utrecht: Desclée de Brouwer, 1963), p. 97, note 1.

14. Pierre Teilhard de Chardin, *The Phenomenon of Man* (New York: Harper & Row, 1959), p. 78.

15. *Ibid.*, pp. 159-160.

16. John Dillenberger, *Protestant Thought and Natural Science, A Historical Interpretation* (London: William Collins Sons, 1961), p. 23.

17. Cf. N. M. Wildiers, *Het Wereldbeeld van Teilhard de Chardin* (Antwerpen-Amsterdam: N. V. Standaard-Boekhandel, 1962), pp. 38 ff.

18. On Teilhard's ideas on God "above" and God "ahead," see *The Future of Man*, Vol. V of his works (New York: Harper & Row, 1964), pp. 306 ff.

19. *Letters from a Traveller*, p. 207.

20. For Teilhard's ideas on the future of man, see *Le Groupe Zoologique Humain* (Paris: Editions Albin Michel, 1956), Chap. 5. Also *L'Avenir de l'Homme*, passim, and particularly pp. 353 ff. It is interesting to note that many existentialist interpretations of man do not take into account his being interwoven with the whole of creation. Nor do they pay any attention to his historical and eschatological fulfillment. (See Chap. 1, above.)

21. *The Divine Milieu*, pp. 127-128.

22. Cf. John Baillie, *The Belief in Progress* (London: Oxford University Press, 1950), pp. 83 ff.

23. *The Divine Milieu*, p. 133.

24. Cf. Teilhard's prayer in the desert, "The Mass on the World," in *Hymn of the Universe* (New York: Harper & Row, 1965), p. 19.

7. Fuller: The World Come of Age: A Second Look at Bonhoeffer

1. See also (in English) Eberhard Bethge's Alden-Tuthill Lectures, "The Challenge of Dietrich Bonhoeffer's Life and Theology," *The Chicago Theological Seminary Register*, Vol. LI, No. 2 (Feb., 1961), pp. 1-38.

2. John Godsey, *The Theology of Dietrich Bonhoeffer* (Philadelphia: The Westminster Press, 1960). This deals with Bonhoeffer's published works to that date, but could not include the later material that has been published in *Gesammelte Schriften*.

3. A. M. Ramsey, "Image Old and New," in J. A. T. Robinson, *The Honest to God Debate* (London: S. C. M. Press, 1963), p. 270.

4. Alasdair MacIntyre, in J. A. T. Robinson, *The Honest to God Debate*, pp. 215-228, especially pp. 215-216.

5. R. P. C. Hanson, in J. A. T. Robinson, *The Honest to God Debate*, p. 109.

6. Alasdair MacIntyre, in J. A. T. Robinson, *The Honest to God Debate*, pp. 221-222.

7. *Ibid.*, p. 222.

8. Nicholls: Christ and Man

1. Karl Barth, *Church Dogmatics*, III/2 (Edinburgh: T. & T. Clark, 1960), pp. 132-133.

2. See *The Christian Century* (Jan. 20, 1960), p. 75.

3. D. M. MacKinnon, "Grammar and Theologic," in *Encounter* (Oct., 1963).

4. Paul Van Buren, *The Secular Meaning of the Gospel* (New York: The Macmillan Co., 1963), p. 98.

5. R. B. Braithwaite, *An Empiricist's View of the Nature of Religious Belief* (Cambridge, Eng.: Cambridge University Press, 1955).

6. Cf. Norman Malcolm, "Anselm's Ontological Arguments," in *Philosophical Review* (Jan., 1960).

7. William Nicholls, "On Living in the Twentieth Century," in David M. Paton (ed.), *Essays in Anglican Self-Criticism* (London: S. C. M. Press, 1958).

8. Marshall McLuhan, *The Gutenberg Galaxy* (Toronto: University of Toronto Press, 1962).

9. Dietrich Bonhoeffer, *Letters and Papers from Prison,* ed. by Eberhard Bethge and trans. by Reginald H. Fuller (London: S. C. M. Press, 1956), pp. 121-122.

Contributors

WILLIAM NICHOLLS, Professor and Head of the Department of Religious Studies, University of British Columbia, Vancouver, Canada.

KEITH R. BRIDSTON, Professor of Systematic Theology, Pacific Lutheran Seminary, Berkeley, California.

D. G. BROWN, Associate Professor of Philosophy, University of British Columbia, Vancouver, Canada.

PIETER DE JONG, Professor of Systematic Theology, St. Andrew's College, Saskatoon, Canada.

REGINALD H. FULLER, Professor of New Testament Language and Literature, Seabury-Western Theological Seminary, Evanston, Illinois.

JAMES M. GUSTAFSON, Professor of Christian Ethics, Yale University Divinity School, and Chairman of the Department of Religious Studies, Yale University.

NATHAN A. SCOTT, JR., Professor of Theology and Literature, Divinity School, University of Chicago.

RONALD GREGOR SMITH, Professor of Divinity, University of Glasgow, Scotland.